太乙金華宗旨

IN THE MEMORY OF DR. MONICA ESPOSITO

Fonts used in this book were Code2000 for both, English and Chinese texts. This edition/translation is based on the Chinese mass paperback version of the original Mandarin text.

The Front Cover's image is from the Changchun Temple ,Master and disciples painting.

I like to thank my translator who chose to remain anonymous. Her diligent translation, expertise in Chinese Taoist alchemy and hard work made this edition possible.
Any questions about content and translations should be directed to Ancient Wisdom Publications.

Editor
http://www.andras-nagy.com

太乙金華宗旨

# THE SECRET OF THE GOLDEN FLOWER

### A MANUAL FOR TAOIST INNER ALCHEMY

## WANG CHONGYANG

ANCIENT WISDOM PUBLICATIONS

WOODLAND, CALIFORNIA

© 2013, Ancient Wisdom Publications

ALL RIGHTS RESERVED. This book contains material protected under International and Federal Copyright Laws and Treaties. Any unauthorized reprint or use of this material is prohibited. No part of this book may be reproduced or transmitted in any form or by any means, electronic or mechanical, including photocopying, recording, or by any information storage and retrieval system without express written permission from the author / publisher.

Library of Congress Control Number: 2013938710

Publisher's Cataloging-in-Publication data

Chongwang, Wang
The Secret of the Golden Flower: a Manual for Taoist Inner Alchemy/written by Wang Chongwang, edited by Nagy, Andras
   p.cm
   translation of: Tai Yi Jin Hua Zong Zhi (《太乙金華宗旨》
   1st Edition
   ISBN 978-1-936690-93-0 (pbk.)
   ISBN 978-1-936690-95-4 (alk. paper)

   1. Spiritual Life (Taoism)　2. Spiritual life (Buddhism)
I. Nagy, Andras　II. Title
2013938710

# Contents

Foreword by the Editor　　9

Chapter 1: The Third Eye 第一章：天心　　11

Chapter 2: Primordial Spirit & Consciousness 第二章：元神、识神　19

Chapter 3: Light Reflex and Observation 第三章：回光守中　27

Chapter 4: Light Reflex and Breathing 第四章：回光调息　39

Chapter 5: Light Reflex and Possible Mistakes and Deviations 第五章：回光差谬　49

Chapter 6: Light Reflex and the Milestones and Confirmatory Experiences 第六章：回光证验　53

Chapter 7: Light Reflex and its Proactive Applications 第七章：回光活法　59

Chapter 8: The Virtuosity of Carefree Living 第八章：逍遥诀 61

Chapter 9: Building Foundation in One Hundred Days 第九章：百日筑基　81

Chapter 10: Light of Nature (Cognition), Light of Consciousness (Recognition) 第十章：性光、识光　85

Chapter 11: The Exchange Between the "yin" and "yang" Energy 第十一章：坎离交媾 93

Chapter 12: The Circulation of Energy 第十二章：周天 95

Chapter 13: Song of life　　101
第十三章：劝世歌 101

The Secret of the Golden Flower
Wang Chongyang
Ancient Wisdom Publications
ISBN-10 1-936690-93-4
ISBN-13 978-1-936690-93-0

"When Laozi was leaving the border of China, the guard at the border prevented him. He said, "I won't allow you to leave the country unless you write something." He must have been a very perceptive man, the guard. The world is in his debt for one of the greatest things that has ever been written -- the Tao Te Ching. There is no other book comparable to it.

Finding no way to avoid it, because the guard wouldn't allow him to go and he wanted to leave the country as fast, as quickly, as possible -- death was coming closer and he wanted to die in the silence of the Himalayas -- compelled to write, he sat in the guard's room for three days and completed the book, Tao Te Ching.

But the first thing that he wrote was, "Tao cannot be said. Once said, it is no more Tao."

You can understand what he means. He is saying that if you read the first statement, there is no need to go any further. "Truth cannot be said. Once said, it is no more true" -- this is his declaration. Now, if you understand that, this book is going to be easy."[1]

---

1     OSHO

## *Foreword by the Editor*

Publishing this new translation is somewhat of a strange experience for me. I have been a student and long time follower of the occult and esoteric. I publish and write esoteric books, study magical systems and embark on spiritual journeys in my dreamscape. Not very long ago, I have discovered the public domain version of the Secret of the Golden Flower, a well known alchemical text first translated to German by Richard Wilhelm.

The Chinese text used by Wilhelm is Zhanran Huizhenzi's edition. The fact is, many other versions of the Golden Flower text exist, all traditionally attributed to the immortal Lü Dongbin. Written down by his disciple, Wang Chongyang. You are reading one of such books.

The definitive author of the Golden Flower is hard to pinpoint. According to the lore; Wang Chongyang, in the summer of 1159 when he was 48, he met two Taoist immortals in a tavern, Zhongli Quan and Lü Dongbin. They have trained him in secret alchemical style of Taoism.

I have decided to publish it as an e-book on as many platforms as I could, despite its wide availability for free. During this time I have discovered its hidden secret to meditation and out of body journeys. No matter which translation you would read - follow the instructions to the letter and practice; you will gain insight and success in visions and possibly in Astral travel.

After publishing the public domain e-book I have stumbled across the website of Dr. Monica Esposito of the Kyoto

University. She was a scholar and aficionado of the East, researching and teaching about Taoist texts of the Ming and Qing periods. On her website she posted the translation of the first three chapters of the Secret of the Golden Flower. She has planned to translate the complete twelve chapters but she only managed to complete the first three. Unfortunately, she had passed away in the Spring of 2011.

For reasons not completely obvious to me, I was compelled to have her work complete and hired a translator and meditation expert in Shanghai, China to help me with this project.

While I secretly envy the academia's effort to disseminate and research ancient texts, I sincerely hope and wish that this translation would have merit, as it is focusing on practical, alchemical applications of the teaching of Lü Dongbin.

Andras Nagy, Editor, 2013, Woodland, California

# Chapter 1: The Third Eye[1] 第一章：天心

1.1 吕祖曰："自然曰道，道无名相，一性而已，一元神而已。

1.1 According to Lü-zu, "dao" was not a tangible phenomenon. It had no name or appearance, just mere nature.[2] Hence, Lü-zu continued stating that "dao" was the universal nature or character, and equivalent to the "primordial spirit".[3]

1.2 性命不可见，寄之天光，天光不可见，寄之两目。

1.2. Similarly, one's life span was also not tangible [in that no one knew how long one could live]. It relied on the intangible "light of heaven". Only our two eyes could show life.

1.3 古来仙真，口口相传，传一得一。

1.3 Since time immemorial, spiritual teachings were orally transmitted.

---

1   The literal meaning of "tian xin, 天心" is heavenly heart. Reading through the text, I realize that this refers an area on our face, which is the focal and starting point for this technique. Thus, instead of naming the title in abstract term of heavenly heart, I have directly used a common term that refers directly to this area on the face itself..

2   In Chinese dictionary, "dao" carried various meanings (when paired up with other Chinese characters) – road, avenue, way, path, track, instrument and method. Further, "dao" also referred to "invisible" or "unwritten" rules or codes of moral conduct.

3   In the original text, the character "one" was used. Here, my interpretation of "one" was in its entirety and universality.

1.4 太上见化，东华递传某，以及南北两宗，全真可为极盛，盛者盛其徒众，衰者衰于心传，以至今日，滥泛极矣！凌替极矣！极则返，故蒙净明许祖，垂慈普度，特立教外别传之旨，接引上根。

1.4 Since the manifestation of the Supreme One until the transmission to me [Lü-zu], the "Quan Zhen Dao, 全真道" clan had grown in numbers, with the north and south sub-clans. However, the rapid expansion in numbers was not in tandem with the teaching transmission, resulting in discipline deterioration. Thus, Xu-zu (from the "Jing Ming, 净明" clan) compassionately stepped out to spread the teaching, not only among clan members, but general public as well. He established the principle of teaching transmission outside clan members to reach out to exceptional spiritual talents.

1.5 闻者千劫难逢，受者一时法会，皆当仰体许祖苦心，必于人伦日用间，立定脚跟，方可修真悟性。

1.5 There was an old saying, "It is a rare occasion to be able to hear pure teaching, it is even rarer for a scholar to reach enlightenment." Hence, everyone should deeply appreciate the enormous contribution by Xu-zu. One must apply the teaching in day-to-day life and in harmonious interaction with others. Only those who could establish themselves in daily practices would have the opportunity to taste the real enlightenment.

1.6 我今叨为度师，先以太乙金华宗旨发明，然后细为开说，太乙者，无上之谓。

1.6 Today, I was honored to be teaching the text "Tai Yi Jin Hua Zong Zi, 太乙金华宗旨". First, let me introduce the text briefly, and would elaborate chapter by chapter subsequently. As the title suggested, this text was described as "tai yi, 太乙" meaning ultimate.

1.7 丹诀总假有为而臻无为，非一超直入之旨。

1.7 Although there were many ways or methods to practice, one would generally need to practice a chosen technique patiently and persistently (in apparent reality) to reach the ultimate reality (a non-actionable state). Thus, there was no one easy, quick solution to penetrate the ultimate realm.[4]

1.8 所传宗旨，直提性功，不落第二法门，所以为妙。

1.8 Unlike the other texts which would first expound on the theoretical or spiritual aspect, this particular text began with the technique itself.

1.9 金华即光也，光是何色？

1.9. Next, the title contained the word "jin hua, 金华", which meant golden light. [The character "hua" in Chinese language carried two meanings — light and flower.] What was the colour of this light?

---

4  The teacher attempted to set out the right expectation responsibly.). [The original text used "有为" and "无为" which literally mean "in action" and "non-action" respectively. Here, my interpretation is apparent reality and ultimate reality.]

1.10 取象于金华，亦秘一光字在内，是先天太乙之真炁，水乡铅只一位者此也。

1.10 Expressing in terms of "jin hua, 金华", this light had the golden bright quality. To understand this light further, one could equate it to the ultimate vitality. In the ancient text, "Ru Yao Jing, 入药镜" written by Cui Xi Fan (late Tang Dynasty, 880 A.C.), a reference to this could be found in the phrase, "shui xiang qian, zhi yi wei, 水乡铅, 只一位", further illustrated this ultimate light. [5]

1.11 回光之功，全用逆法，注想天心，天心居日月中。

1.11 In order to accomplish the light reflex, one would focus its attention on the third eye, located between two eyes.

1.12 《黄庭经》云：'寸田尺宅可治生'，尺宅面也。面上寸田，非天心而何？

1.12 In another ancient text, "Huang Ting Jing, 黄庭经" written by the famous calligrapher, politician and strategist, Wang Xi Yi (365 A. C..), There was a description about a specific area on our face that could regulate life This is none other than the third eye.[6]

---

[5] As this phrase is one of the forty-four phrases in this entire text of "Ru Yao Jing", my take is that it would be meaningless to translate without the context therein. Thus, leaving the phrase in pin yin as is. One underlying condition to remember is that the teacher was talking to students, presumably with "dao" background. Such reference would be mentioned in passing to reinforce the point made. For our purpose, the understanding of light as the ultimate vitality suffices for now.

[6] Instead of translating as a question as posed by the teacher, "What

1.13 方寸中具有郁罗肖台之胜，玉京丹阙之奇，乃至虚至灵之神所住。

1.13 The third eye was likened to be the splendid spiritual residence.

1.14 儒曰：'虚中'；释曰：'灵台'；道曰：'祖土'、曰'黄庭'、曰'玄关'、曰'先天窍'。

1.14 Confucius referred to it as the central void ("xu zhong, 虚中"). Buddha Sakyamuni referred to it as the soul platform ("ling tai, 灵台"). Taoist had many references, including, the ancestral soil ("zu tu, 祖土"), the yellow courtyard ("huang ting, 黄庭"), the mysterious pass ("xuan guan, 玄关" and the innate opening / aperture ("xian tian qiao, 先天窍").[7]

1.15 盖天心犹宅舍一般，光乃主人翁也。

1.15 In short, the light dwells in the third eye.

1.16 故一回光，周身之炁皆上朝，如圣王定都立极，执玉帛者万国；又如主人精明，奴婢自然奉命，各司其事。

1.16 Once the light reflex started, all the bodily energy would gather upward at the top of the head, just like a could it be other than the third eye?", I have translated the sentence into a statement instead.

7　　In Chinese language, there are many terms for the third eye. Here, I used direct translation to reflect the various terms (without explaining the context of each). For our purpose, the key is to know that the area of focus in this technique starts with the third eye.

mighty king receiving tributes from all nations at the capital city. Similarly, just like an astute master, the servants would naturally obey its leader.

1.17 诸子只去回光，便是无上妙谛。

1.17 Therefore, practising the technique to realize the light reflex was the ultimate purpose here.

1.18 光易动而难定，回之既久，此光凝结，即是自然法身，而凝神于九霄之上矣。

1.18 However, one should note that the light was restless. With the light reflex practice, the light could be sustained longer, leading to the natural revelation of the ultimate self and finally reaching the state of heavenly rapture.

1.19 《心印经》所谓'默朝飞升者此也'。

1.19 This same state was described very aptly in the Buddhist ancient text, "Xin Yin Jing, 心印经", written during the Tang Dynasty.

1.20 宗旨行去，别无求进之法，只在纯想于此。

1.20 Focusing the attention on the third eye was the only way to practise this technique.

1.21 《楞严经》云：'纯想即飞，必生天上，天非苍苍之天，即生身于乾宫是也。久之，自然身外有身。'

1.21 Another Buddhist ancient text, "Leng Yan Jing, 楞严经" (Tang Dynasty, 705 A.C.) expounded that focused, meditative practice could lead to mind purification and enlightenment. It described the process as "flying" or ascending to the "sky". Here, the "sky" was not the physical "blue sky", but the top of our head. With sustained focus, the ultimate self would reveal itself naturally.

1.22 金华即金丹，神明变化，各师于心，此种妙诀，虽不差毫末，然而甚活，全要聪明，又须沉静，非极聪明人行不得，非极沉静人守不得。"

1.22 Further, "jin hua, 金华" (golden light) could be equated to "jin dan, 金丹" (literally meaning golden pill, which was equivalent to the pill of immortality.) It could adapt individually to different states of mind. While the instructions remained the same for everyone, its application and efficacy could vary flexibly. An ideal practitioner must possess both a penetrating and a calm mind. Without a penetrating mind, one could not apply the technique effectively. Without a calm mind, one could not sustain the practice as required by the technique.

# Chapter 2: Primordial Spirit & Consciousness 第二章：元神、识神

2.1 吕祖曰："天地视人如蜉蝣，大道视天地亦泡影。

2.1 Lü-zu taught, "In the eyes of the universe, human being was like a mayfly (a peculiar kind of insect, which lived for only one day, and would lose its ability to eat upon maturity). Likewise, within the context of "dao" (ultimate truth), the universe was just as temporal."

2.2 惟元神真性，则超元会而上之。

2.2 Only the primordial spirit would last forever.

2.3 其精气则随天地而败坏矣。

2.3 Whereas human was mere mortal, its essence and energy of life would deteriorate, in line with the temporal nature of the universe.

2.4 然有元神在，即无极也。生天生地皆由此矣。

2.4 The very existence of the primordial spirit proved the phenomenon of infinity[8], where the universe came into its existence. [9]

---

8    A core that remained in our transient world. (First choice of the word was literally "ultimacy"[editor]). The usage or words of ultimacy or infinity is trying to describe the concept of a supreme order for all things (Tao).
9    In the Chinese context, "wu ji, 无极" describes to

2.5 能守护元神，则超生在阴阳之外，不在三界之中，此惟见性方可，所谓本来面目也。

2.5 Therefore, the primary objective for a "dao" practitioner is to safeguard and preserve the primordial spirit, which could lead to enlightenment beyond the Samsaric wheel of life. In this regard, one must penetrate and fully realize the true nature of being, i.e. the ultimate self or reality.

2.6 凡人投胎时，元神居方寸，而识神则居下心。下面血肉心，形如大桃，有肺以覆翼之，肝佐之，大小肠承之，假如一日不食，心上便大不自在，至闻惊而跳，闻怒而闷，见死亡则悲，见美色则眩，头上天心何尝微微些动也。

2.6 Since human birth, the primordial spirit resided in the third eye, whereas the consciousness resided in the heart, a peach-shape flesh and blood [in other word, physical] organ, with assistance and support from the liver and digestive system [the text mentioned the intestines]. If a man did not eat for one day, the heart would not feel at ease. When shocking news was heard, the heart would throb intensely. When hearing fury words, the heart would feel stifled. When seeing death, the heart would feel sad or in grief. When seeing beauty, the heart would be dazzled. But, the third eye never moved, not even slightly.

---

phenomenon of boundlessness, something beyond apparent reality. Here, both Taoism and Buddhism share the view of ultimate truth / reality, but the Chinese use of word can be hard to translate and confusing. "wu" means none and "ji" means utmost (some kind of boundary), thus "wu ji" put together connotes something beyond boundary. I have chosen to translate into "infinity" rather than "boundlessness" as I think it is more understandable in the western context..

2.7 问天心不能动乎？。

2.7 If one asked, "Could the third eye not move?"

2.8 方寸中之真意，如何能动。

2.8 If the true nature (or ultimate self, i.e. the primordial spirit) truly resided in the third eye, how could it move?

2.9 到动时便不妙，然亦最妙，凡人死时方动，此为不妙；最妙者，光已凝结为法身，渐渐灵通欲动矣，此千古不传之秘也。

2.9 If it moved, that would be far from good at the apparent level, as only at the point of death, the third eye would move [leaving this body to the next]. But, with practice, if one had managed to sustain the light (as explained in Chapter 1) such that the true nature or the ultimate self revealed itself, the third eye would start to move wonderfully. This is the eternal truth from thousands of years ago.

2.10 丹道，以精水、神火、意土三者，为无上之诀。

2.10 The consciousness was likened to a strong, aggressive warrior, who took advantage of the "weakness" of the "sovereign king" (i.e. the primordial spirit, which resided in the third eye). Over time, it had taken over the "throne". [10]

10  Here, I think the teacher is trying to describe the current body and mind predicament where we are not aware of the ultimate self, but bound within the constraint of our bodily structure..

2.11 今凝守元宫，如英明之主在上，二目回光，如左右大臣尽心辅弼，内政既肃，自然一切奸雄，无不倒戈乞命矣。

2.11 Once the rightful owner of the third eye (i.e. the primordial spirit) returned to its rightful position (rightly realized and penetrated), it was as if the wise and brilliant "sovereign king" presided over the reign. At the state of light reflex, the two eyes would become the left and right courtiers who gave full support to their ruler, cleaning up its acts and domestic affairs [Alternative: putting its house in order]. Naturally, the treacherous one would raise "white flag" and surrender accordingly.

2.12 丹道，以精水、神火、意土三者，为无上之诀。

2. 12 In the pursuit of immortality,[11] there were 3 crucial elements — essence (water element), spirit (fire element) and mind (or thought) (earth element).[12]

2.13 精水云何？乃先天真一之炁，神火即光也，意土即中宫天心也。

---

[11] In the Chinese context, this has a historical reference to the elixir of life.
[12] Essence – referring to breath, energy and bodily fluid (in traditional Chinese medicine, when one is ill, the prescription of medication generally addresses this essence which is not in balance, causing illnesses. Spirit here covers a more general meaning, not only primordial spirit. Mind is a tricky translation. In many ways, it may be synonymous to consciousness, but I have used consciousness for "shi 识" (knowledge, in conscious state of mind). "Yi意" on the other hand connotes both conscious and unconscious states of mind, more to mean thought, intent, desire, want, craving. I used the word "mind" for its neutrality..

2.13 What was essence? It referred to energy of life. [In Taoism, it is believed that the human life originates from this energy of life.] Spirit referred to light. Mind / thought referred to both the chest / heart area (middle "dan tian", an acupoint on the body) and the third eye.[13]

2.14 以神火为用，意土为体，精水为基。

2.14 The three elements worked together where the spirit fired up life, with the mind as the body and the essence as the body's foundation.

2.15 凡人以意生身，身不止七尺者为身也。盖身中有魄焉，魄附识而用，识依魄而生。魄阴也，识之体也，识不断，则生生世世，魄之变形易质无已也。

2.15 The human body was a derivation of mind. Here, not only it referred to the 7 feet flesh and blood structure, it comprised the soul, i.e. anima (feminine) and animus (masculine) as well.[14] Anima was embodied in consciousness. So long as consciousness remained, one would be roll unceasingly from life to life. Anima would continue to be attached to consciousness, regardless of body.

2.16 惟有魂，神之所藏也。魂昼寓于目，夜舍于肝，寓目而视，舍肝而梦，梦者神游也，九天九地，刹那历遍。觉则冥冥焉，渊渊焉，拘于形也，即拘于魄也。

2.16 On the other hand, animus was embodied in spirit.

---

13    Both conscious and unconscious mind.
14    This is another tricky translation – "hun, 魂", "po, 魄" and "hun po" combined all mean soul. But, "po" is the "yin" and and "hun" is the "yang" aspects of soul. Here, I applied the feminine anima for the "yin" soul and the masculine animus for the "yang" soul

It resided in the eyes during day time and liver in the night time. In the eyes, men could see. In the liver, men could dream. Dreaming was the act where the spirit wondered. However, one could not remember the dreams after awaken, because of the constraints of the body and anima.

2.17 故回光所以炼魂，即所以保神，即所以制魄，即所以断识。

2.17 Therefore, the purpose of practising light reflex was to refine the animus. In doing so, the spirit would be safeguard. The anima would be subjugated and the consciousness could cease.

2.18 古人出世法，炼尽阴滓，以返纯乾，不过消魄全魂耳。

2.18 The wise sage in the past taught one to remove all the impurities in order to reach the state of enlightenment. This essentially meant that one would have to eliminate the anima and preserve the animus.

2.19 回光者，消阴制魄之诀也，虽无返乾之功，止有回光之诀，光即乾也，回之即返之也。

2.19 The light reflex practice was meant to eliminate and subjugate the anima. Though there was no mention about the path to enlightenment, the state of light reflex actually meant the state of enlightenment.

2.20 只守此法，自然精水充足，神火发生，意土凝定，而圣胎可结矣。

2.20 Practising this technique persistently would naturally ensure that the essence would be abundantly available, the spirit fire would continue and the mind became still and calm. This would lead to becoming a noble being.

2.21 蜣螂转丸，而丸中生白，神注之纯功也。粪丸中尚可生胎离壳，而吾天心休息处，注神于此，安得不生身乎。

2.21 As an analogy, one could observe the dung beetle, which continually rubbed and rolled in the dung, until a white protective material was produced. This was the power of concentration. Even an insect could survive and multiply in the dung, there would be no reason for men not to achieve enlightenment, if proper concentration was given to the primordial spirit in the third eye.

2.21 一灵真性，既落乾宫，便分魂魄。魂在天心，阳也，轻清之炁也，此自太虚得来，与元始同形。

2.22 The true nature of the ultimate self is split into anima and animus. Animus, dwelled in the third eye as well, was the "yang" soul, with a quality of lightness and purity, which came from the universe, and shared similar form as the primordial spirit from the beginning of time.

2.23 魄阴也，沉浊之气也，附于有形之凡心。

2.23 Anima was the "yin" soul, with a quality of darkness and impurity, which was enslaved in the worldly desire.

2.24 魂好生，魄望死。

2.24 Animus seeks life, whereas anima seeks death.

2.25 一切好色动气皆魄之所为，即识神也。

2.25 All the worldly afflictions came from anima. Thus, anima is equivalent to the consciousness.

2.26 死后享血食，活则大苦，阴返阴也。 物以类聚也。

2.26 For anima, life was a distress and suffering. After death, it could feed on blood. It could return to its rightful place of belonging, the "yin" realm.

2.27 学人炼尽阴魄，即为纯阳也。"

2.27 In conclusion, the practitioner would just need to focus on eliminating the anima. This would naturally lead to the state of enlightenment.

# Chapter 3: Light Reflex and Observation 第三章：回光守中

3.1 吕祖曰："回光之名何昉乎？昉之自文始真人也。

3.1 Lü-zu asked, "Do you know who coined the term, "light reflex"? It was first mentioned in "Guan Yin Zi, 关尹子", one of the Taoist ancient texts, written by "Guan Yin Zi" himself during Song Dynasty (960 — 1279 A. C..).[15]

3.2 回光则天地阴阳之气无不凝，所谓精思者此也，纯炁者此也，纯想者此也。

3.2 When light reflex was achieved, all the "yin" and "yang" energy of the universe would agglomerate. Other terms such as "thought penetration / refinement / virtuosity" and "energy purification" referred to the same phenomenon.[16]

---

15  In the old days, the Chinese typically named its text by the author, just like Lao Zi who wrote the "Lao Zi" text. Similarly, the text "Guan Yin Zi" was authored by "Guan Yin Zi" and is considered as one of the main texts for Chinese philosophy. Guan was an ardent student of Lao Zi, and this text documented his understanding and wisdom of Lao Zi's proposition of "dao".

16  Here, the teacher draw parallel to 3 terms "hui guang, 回光" (relating to light), "jing si, 精思" (relating to thought) and "chun qi, 纯气" (relating to energy). Here, the Chinese term are formed with adjective/verb + noun. In the English translation, I have used "light reflex" (noun + noun) for "hui guang" (literally means "hui" return / reflect and "guang" means light). Following the same pattern, I have tentatively translated "jing si" and "chun qi" in the same way.

3.3 初行此诀，乃有中似无，久之功成，身外有身，乃无中似有。

3.3 When one began to practise, it felt as if nothing could be perceived (within the body structure). Over time, as one gained mastery of the technique, one could perceived everything (out of nothing), achieving the state of ultimate self (alongside the apparent self).

3.4 百日专功，光才真，方为神火。

3.4 In this regard, one had to work hard with full concentration (for 100 days consecutively) so that the "real" light could be realized, penetrating the actual spirit within.

3.5 百日后，光中自然一点真阳，忽生黍珠，如夫妇交合有胎，便当静以待之，光之回，即火候也。

3.5 After the hundredth day, the agglomerated light would naturally become the genuine "yang" energy within the human body, in the form of corn-shape pearl. The process was like the embryo formation as the result of conception between the husband and wife. One would have to calmly await to reach such state. Here, there might be different degree of light intensity.

3.6 夫元化之中，有阳光为主宰，有形者为日，在人为目，走漏神识，莫此甚顺也。

3.6 It was widely acknowledged that the creation process was predominantly dictated by the light ("yang" natured). In the physical world, it was represented by the sun. In the human body structure, it would be the two eyes, through which the spirit and consciousness could habitually move about.

3.7 故金华之道，全用逆法。回光者，非回一身之精华，直回造化之真炁，非止一时之妄念，直空千劫之轮回。故一息当一年，人间时刻也，一息当百年，九途长夜也。

3.7 However, in this "jin hua" (golden light / flower) technique, this habitual pattern would be broken away. That was why the technique was referred to as a reversal method. [In fact, light reflex connotes the same phenomenon.] To summarize, the objective of light reflex was not only to recover the essence of being, but to recover the entire flow of energy at the creation process. It was not only to stem out the delusional thoughts, but to release one from the wheel of Samsaric life. The wheel of life followed every being like breathing. Every breath taken was considered as one year according to human reckoning, and 100 years accordingly to the realm of the dead.

3.8 凡人自 的一声之后，逐境顺生，至老未尝逆视，阳气衰灭，便是九幽之界。

3.8 Since birth, man had lived within the habitual pattern of an impure life. Even after maturity, one had not tried this reverse insight. Hence, the "yang" energy flow continued to deteriorate. When fully depleted, one reached the realm of the dead (with 100% "yin" energy flow).

3.9 故《楞严经》云：'纯想即飞，纯情即坠'。学人想少情多，沉沦下道。

3.9 The Buddhist ancient text, "Leng Yan Jing" (Tang Dynasty, 705 A.C.) [which was mentioned in Chapter one as well] taught that "pure mind led to enlightenment, pure desire led to destruction" [or may be "suffering" could be more appropriate for the word "destruction"]. A "dao" practitioner, who indulged more in worldly desire and less in purifying the mind, would succumb to the path of suffering.

3.10 惟谛观息静便成正觉，用逆法也。

3.10 Only through the reversal method of inner self searching and contemplative meditation, one could realize the right awareness.[17]

3.11 《阴符经》云：'机在目'。《黄帝素问》云：'人身精华，皆上注于空窍是也。'

3.11 In the "dao" ancient text, "Yin Fu Jing, 阴符经" [Year of origin still a mystery, some believe that the text was written as early as 300 B.C and some believe it was written in Tang Dynasty (618 – 907 A.C.)], the importance of eyes was highlighted. On the other hand, the ancient Chinese medical text, "Huang Di Su Wen, 黄帝素问", had similar record that the essence of being could be unlocked through "emptying" the apertures of the body.

3.12 得此一节，长生者在兹，超升者亦在兹矣。此是贯彻三教工夫。

3.12 From this chapter, one could obtain the principle of immortality and enlightenment. This was common for all the main teaching of Confucius, Buddhism and Taoism.

---

17    Similar to the Buddhist noble eight-fold path.

3.13 光不在身中，亦不在身外，山河大地，日月照临，无非此光，故不独在身中。聪明智慧，一切运转，亦无非此光，所以亦在身外。

3.13 The light was neither inside nor outside the body. For example, the earth received light from the sun and the moon. Thus, the light was not inside the earth. But, in order for the earth to rotate and function properly, it depended on the lights of the sun and moon, which meant that the light could not be outside the earth either.

3.14 天地之光华，布满大千，一身之光华，亦自漫天盖地，所以一回光，天地山河一切皆回矣。

3.14 Similarly, the light of the universe permeated all corners of the universe. The light of being would have the same effect as well. Once the state of light reflex was achieved, all things on earth would return to its ultimate state.

3.15 人之精华，上注于目，此人身之大关键也。

3.15 In order to realize the essence of being, one would focus on the eyes.

3.16 子辈思之，一日不静坐，此光流转，何所底止！若一刻能静坐，万劫千生，从此了彻。万法归于静，真不可思议，此妙谛也。

3.16 Just imagine, without practising meditation, the light would not be retained but would continue to flow out. With meditation, the root of suffering in Samsaric life could be eliminated all together. This was a powerful

3.17然工夫下手，由浅入深，由粗入细，总以不间断为妙。

3.17 For a practitioner to gain mastery of the technique, the most important attitude was to learn and practise persistently.

3.18工夫始终则一，但其间冷暖自知，要归于天空海阔，万法如如，方为得手。

3.18 While the technique remained the same throughout, the process for each practitioner would differ. Only the practitioner himself would know his own progress. In any case, one would have gained mastery of the technique upon the realization of the ultimate truth.

3.19 圣圣相传，不离反照。孔云：'致知'，释曰：'观心'，老云：'内观'，皆此法也。

3.19 All the teachings from the saints and sages of the past revolved around inner-self reflection and contemplation. Confucius taught about the "ultimate knowing". Buddha Sakyamuni taught about the "contemplative heart". Lao Zi also taught about the "inner contemplation". All pointed to the same direction.

3.20 但反照二字，人人能言，不能得手，未识二字之义耳。

3.20 Everyone seemed to know about self-reflection and contemplation somewhat, but very few had mastery over it. Most would claim that they would self-reflect and contemplate, without properly understanding the actual meaning of self-reflection and contemplation.

3.21 反者，自知觉之心，反乎形神未兆之初，则吾六尺之中，反求个天地未生之体。

3.21 Here, the real purpose of self-reflection and contemplation was to penetratingly lead one to the ultimate self.

3.22 今人但一、二时中间静坐，反顾己私，便云反照，安得到头！

3.22 However, many "dao" practitioners today would claim of self-reflection and contemplation after one to two hours of meditation. How untruthful!

3.23 佛道二祖，教人看鼻尖者，非谓着念于鼻端也。亦非谓眼观鼻端，念又注中黄也。

3.23 Both founders of Buddhism and Taoism taught about the observation of the nose tip. This neither meant that one should concentrate all thoughts at the nose tip nor one should place the eyes, gazing at the nose tip while concentrating all thoughts at the diaphragm.

3.24 眼之所至，心亦至焉，何能一上而一下也，又何能忽上而忽下也。此皆误指而为月。

3.24 The truth is: wherever the eyes gazed, the thoughts would follow. Thus, it would not be possible to separate the two.

3.25 初不在鼻上，盖以大开眼，则视远，而不见鼻矣。太闭眼。则眼合，亦不见鼻矣。大开失之外走，易于散乱。太闭失之内驰，易于昏沉。惟垂帘得中，恰好望见鼻端，故取以为准。只是垂帘恰好，任彼光自然透入，不劳你注射与不注射。

3.25 The real purpose of observing the nose tip was to place the eyes properly. When sitting down to meditate, one should keep the eyes half closed. If the eyes were wide opened, one would get distracted easily. On the other hand, if the eyes were completely shut, one would get drowsy easily as well. Here, the nose tip became a helpful guide. If the eyes were wide opened, one would not see the nose tip. If the eyes were completely shut, again, one would not see the nose tip. Only when the eyes were half closed, one could see the nose tip.

3.26 看鼻端，只于最初入静处举眼一视，定个准则便放下。

3.26 The point to note was that one needed to only observe the nose tip at the beginning of meditation. Once the eyes and gaze were fixed, one could disregard it accordingly.

3.27 如泥水匠人用线一般，彼自起手一挂，便依了做上去，不只管把线看也。

3.27 An analogy was how a mason would hang some guiding strings to build a wall. The mason need not observe the strings all the time as the wall was built.

3.28 止观是佛法，原不秘的。

3.28 It is no secret that contemplative meditation (samantha and vipassana) originated from the Buddhist practice.

3.29 以两目谛观鼻端正身安坐，系心缘中，不必言头中，但于两〇中间齐平处系念便了。

3.29 The meditation practice required one to sit in upright position, with both eyes gazing at the nose tip. This would suffice to calm oneself. Next, one would fix the thoughts at the third eye area.

3.30 光是活泼泼的东西，系念两〇中间，光自然透入，不必著意于中宫也，此数语已括尽要旨。其余入静出静前后，以下止观书印证可也。

3.30 Light is restless. When the thoughts were fixed at the third eye area, light might stream in. But there was no need to direct the attention elsewhere. Here, I have expounded on the key instruction for this meditation practice. For the remaining meditation steps, the Buddhist text of contemplative meditation ("Zhi Guan Shu, 止观书") could be used as the reference.

3.31 缘中二字极妙。中无不在，遍大千皆在里许，聊指造化之机，缘此入门耳。缘者缘此为端倪，非有定著也，此二字之义，活甚妙甚。

3.31 The Buddhist term, "yuan zhong, 缘中" was wonderful indeed. The word "zhong, 中" (literal meaning, "centre or middle") meant that it was an omnipresent phenomenon, which included the universe of existence. This was where "yuan" (literal meaning, "condition") would make its entry.

3.32 止观二字，原离不得，即定慧也。

3.32 The words "zhi, 止" (samatha) and "guan, 观" (vipassana) could not be separated as well. They referred to "concentration" and "wisdom" respectively.

3.33 以后凡念起时，不要仍旧兀坐，当究此念在何处，从何起，从何灭，反复推究，了不可得。即见此念起处也，不要又讨过起处，觅心了不可得。吾与汝安心竟，此是止观，反此者，名为邪观。

3.33 During meditation, if worldly thoughts arose, one might investigate and examine from where the thoughts originated, to where the thoughts disappeared. But, to be sitting still and examining the origination and passing away of each thought could lead to a pointless process. Here, the ideal for right meditation was to balance between concentration and wisdom.

3.34 如是不可得已，即仍旧绵绵去止，而继之以观，观而继之以止，是定慧双修，此为回光。

3.34 When thoughts arose, one would stop concentrating (i.e. samatha) to apply vipassana (i.e. gaining wisdom). After a while, one would switched back to samatha. This technique allowed for practice of both concentration and wisdom. This was in line with the state of light reflex.

3.35 回者止也，光者观也。止而不观，名为有回而无光；观而不止，名为有光而无回，志之。"

3.35 Here, the light referred to vipassana (i.e. wisdom) and reflect meant samatha (i.e. concentration). Please be reminded that with only concentration, without wisdom, it was as if there was reflex without light, whereas with only wisdom, without concentration, it was equivalent to having light but no reflex.

# Chapter 4: Light Reflex and Breathing 第四章：回光调息

4.1 吕祖曰："宗旨只要纯心行去，不求验而验自至。

4.1 According to Lü-zu, "As long as one practised the technique in a persistent and focused manner, the results would naturally ensue. If, however, one practised with desire to achieve certain results, the benefits of this technique might allude oneself.

4.2 大约初机病痛，昏沉散乱，二种尽之。

4.2 In general, there were two problems (here, the text called the problem as an "illness") for the beginners — drowsiness and distraction.

4.3 却此有机窍，无过寄心于息，息者自心也。自心为息，心一动，而即有气，气本心之化也。

4.3 In order to address these problems, one would have to put emphasis on breathing. To elaborate, breathing was the gateway to the mind. Pictorially, the Chinese character of "xi, 息" (breathing) was formed by combining two Chinese characters, "zi, 自" (self) and "xin, 心" (heart). Hence, Chinese had a saying that breathing is the reflection of one's heart / mind. Any movement of the mind, there would be a corresponding breath.

4.4 吾人念至速，霎顷一妄念，即一呼吸应之。故内呼吸与外呼吸，如声响之相随，一日有几万息，即有几万妄念。神明漏尽，如木槁灰死矣。

4.4 Whenever a thought arose, it would become a fleeting thought within a split of moment. With every fleeting thought, a breath followed. Thus, thought was like the inner breath of the mind whereas breath was the outer representation of the mind. Both thought and breath were like sound and echo, following each other closely. In one day, one would take many breathes, meaning many thoughts arose in mind. Over time, the spirit of man would be depleted, leading to death.

4.5 然则欲无念乎，不能无念也，欲无息乎，不能无息也。莫若即其病而为药，则心息相依是已。

4.5 In that case, why not just stop all the thoughts from arising? That was not possible. It would be as if one would stop breathing, something impossible to do. In order to address the two problems of drowsiness and distraction (here, the text used the term "cure the illnesses"), one could apply this "medicine" (or prescription) of uniting the breath and mind.

4.6 故回光兼之以调息，此法全用耳光。一是目光，一是耳光。目光者，外日月交光也，耳光者，内日月交精也。

4.6 Therefore, during the state of light reflex, one would need to regulate the breathing as well. Light reflex could be observed through sight, whereas breathing could be observed through sound. Here, both the eyes sense door (sight) and the ears sense door (sound) were used to penetrate the ultimate truth (at the spiritual level) and the apparent truth (at the essence level) respectively. [With reference to Chapter 2]

4.7 然精即光之凝定处，同出而异名也。

4.7 In a nutshell, the essence (i.e. the energy of life) was equivalent to the state of light agglomeration. Both were different terms but referring to the same phenomenon.

4.8 故聪明总一灵光而已。

4.8 Colloquially, one was described as "ling guang, 灵光" (literal meaning "effective light") if one was deemed to have a penetrating mind. [With reference to Chapter 1]

4.9 坐时用目垂帘后，定个准则便放下。然竟放下，又恐不能，即存心于听息。

4.9 When sitting down to meditate with eyes half closed, one would try to relax the mind (the text used the term "fang xia, 放下" which meant "let go"). But it might not be possible to just relax immediately. In this case, one could fix the mind on the sound / rhythm of breath as transition.

4.10 息之出入，不可使耳闻，听惟听其无声也。一有声，便粗浮而不入细，即耐心轻轻微微些，愈放愈微，愈微愈静，久之，忽然微者遽断，此则真息现前，而心体可识矣。

4.10 When breathing, one should not hear the sound of breath, but to be aware of the inhaling and exhaling. If the sound of breath could be heard, it meant that the breath was still coarse (reflecting a gross mind). In this regard, one should focus patiently to reach softer and softer breath (and hence a subtler and subtler mind), until it reached a state as though the physical breath had stopped. At that time, one would be sustained by the "true breathing", enabling the mind to penetrate the ultimate truth.

4.11 盖心细则息细，心一则动炁也，息细则心细，炁一则动心也。

4.11 Once the mind became subtle, the breath would correspondingly become soft. With a focused mind, one could mobilize [for the translation of "dong, 动"] the "true breathing". Further, the soft breath could enable an even subtler mind. With a steady breath, one could influence [also for the translation of "dong, 动"] the state of mind.

4.12 定心必先之以养炁者，亦以心无处入手，故缘炁为之端倪，所谓纯炁之守也。

4.12 Teachers of the past advocated that before steadying the mind, one would have to first cultivate the energy of life (i.e. accessing the essence via the ears sense door). The objective was to use the breath as the gateway (or "bridge") to penetrate the mind.

4.13 子辈不明动字，动者以线索牵动言，即制字之别名也。

4.13 Many students might not understand the meaning of "mobilize" or "influence" (see the above). Both mind and breath were inter-linked, as like thread pulling each other to reach for higher level of penetration.

4.14 即可以奔趋使之动，独不可以纯静使之宁乎。

4.14 In the physical world, one would use a thread to pull another still object to move. Similarly, it would be impossible to silent the mind without any tool.

4.15 此大圣人，视心炁之交，而善立方便，以惠后人也。

4.15 The saints and sages of the past had observed this very important connection between mind and breath. As the result, we could benefit by adopting this breath technique.

4.16 丹书云：'鸡能抱卵常听'，此要诀也。盖鸡之所以能生卵者，以暖气也。暖气止能温其壳，不能入其中，则以心引炁入，其听也，一心注焉，心入则气入，得暖气而生矣。故母鸡虽有时出外，而常作侧耳势，其神之所注未常少间也。神之所注，未尝少间，即暖气亦昼夜无间，而神活矣。

4.16 In ancient texts about the pursuit of immorality, there was a wonderfully apt analogy relating to the process of hatching the eggs by hens. Here, it was observed that when the hen hatched her eggs, it not only used the heat of the body to warm the egg shells, it also used the mind concentration to lead the heat into the eggs. Mother hen would listen attentively to her eggs, with full concentration. When the mind entered the eggs, the heat (i.e. the energy of life) would follow and lives began in the eggs. It was further observed that during hatching, the hen might leave its nest for a walk outside, but it would be on high alert listening to its nest. The hen's mind would continually focus on the eggs, awakening the primordial spirit.

4.17 神活者，由其心之先死也。人能死心，元神活矣。

4.17 When primordial spirit was awakened, it marked the death of worldly desires. (The text used the term "si xin, 死心" which literally means the "death of the heart") [Refer to Chapter 2 on anima and animus as well]

4.18 死心非枯槁之谓，乃专一不二之谓也。

4.18 In this context, the "death of the heart" did not refer to the physical death of the heart organ, but it meant to end of worldly thoughts or desires that stirred the mind constantly. Once the worldly thoughts or desires ceased, the mind became concentrated and still.

4.19 佛云：'置心一处，无事不办。'

4.19 Buddha once said, "When mind was single-pointedly concentrated, nothing would be impossible." (In the Buddhist context, this means that even enlightenment was possible.)

4.20 心易走，即以炁纯之，炁易粗，即以心细之，如此而焉有不定者乎？

4.20 The Mind was fickle and restless. The breath was a key tool to calm and still it. But, when the breath was coarse, the mind was used to soften it. Following this technique, the mind can certainly be calmed.[18]

4.21 大约昏沉、散乱二病，散乱者，神驰也，昏沉者，神未清

---
18   The teacher ended here with a question, how not possible for the mind to calm down if the technique of mind-breath is used to benefit each other? I chose to translate it into a statement instead for clarity..

也，散乱易治，而昏沉难医。

4.21 Now, let us return to the two problems of drowsiness and distraction. Comparing the two, distraction would be easier to address than drowsiness. When one became distracted, one would at least have the awareness to realize such distraction. But in the state of drowsiness, one would not even have any awareness of sort.

4.22 譬之病焉，有痛有痒者，药之可也，昏沉则麻木不仁之症也。

4.22 It was as though when one was ill, one would be aware of the pain and discomfort. A medicine could be prescribed to cure the illness. But, drowsiness was like a "numb symptom", difficult to be pin-pointed, hence not easy to cure.

4.23 散者可以收之，乱者可以整之，若昏沉，则蠢蠢焉，冥冥焉。

4.23 There were tow detailed aspects of distraction — mind dispersion and mind disorder. Both could be curbed accordingly. However, if one was in state of drowsiness, the mind was dull.

4.24 散乱尚有方所，至昏沉全是魄用事也。散乱尚有魂在，至昏沉则纯阴为主矣。

4.24 Another difference between distraction and drowsiness was that drowsiness was controlled by anima (the "yin" soul) whereas distraction occurred with the presence of animus (the "yang" soul).

4.25 静坐时欲睡去，便是昏沉。

4.25 When one fell asleep during sitting meditation, one would be in the state of drowsiness.

4.26 却昏沉，只在调息，息即口鼻出入之息，虽非真息，而真息之出入，亦于此寄焉。

4.26 In order to eradicate the drowsiness, one could regulate the breath intentionally, by inhaling through the nose and exhaling through the mouth. Even though, this was not the "true breathing" (as explained above), the "true breath" was embedded in such inhalation and exhalation.

4.27 凡坐须要静心纯气，心何以静，用在息上，息之出入，惟心自知，不可使耳闻，不闻则细，细则清，闻则气粗，粗则浊，浊则昏沉而欲睡，自然之理也。

4.27. When sitting down to meditate, one must calm the mind and soften / refine the breath. In order to calm the mind, one would focus on the breath. Here, the mind would be alert enough to be aware of the soft breath. If one heard his own breath, it meant that the breath was coarse, which would naturally lead to drowsiness.

4.28 虽然心用在息上，又善要会用，亦是不用之用，只要微微照听可耳。此句有微义，何谓照？

4.28 When the mind was applied on the breathing, it should be done properly. In this case, the application was gentle, not overly deliberate. What does this mean?

4.29 即眼光自照。目惟内视而不外视，不外视而惺然者，即内视也，非实有内视。

4.29 Here, the eyes sense door would observe inward. One who was alert and not seeing the surrounding, was deemed to be observing inwardly.

4.30 何谓听？

4.30 What about the ears sense door?

4.31 即耳光自听，耳惟内听而不外听，不外听而惺然者，即内听也，非实有内听。

4.31 Similarly, the ears sense door would listen to the inner self as well. One who was alert and not listening to his surrounding, was deemed to be listening inwardly.

4.32 听者听其无声，视者视其无形。

4.32 In short, one would hear no sound and see no shape.

4.33 目不外视，耳不外听，则闭而欲内驰。惟内视内听，则既不外走，又不内驰，而中不昏沉矣，此即日月交精交光也。

4.33 When one stopped seeing and listening to the surrounding, the distraction could be contained within. Once one achieved the state of inward mind observation (when the eyes sense door observed inward) and inward listening (when the ears sense door listened inward), the distraction could be totally curbed. Further, if the awareness was maintained without falling into the state of drowsiness, the mind would ready to penetrate and realize the ultimate and apparent truth.

4.34 昏沉欲睡，即起散步，神清再坐。

4.34 If one felt drowsy and sleepy, one could stand up to take a walk, and return to meditate when the mind was clear and alert.

4.35 清晨有暇，坐一炷香为妙。

4.35 Every morning, it would be recommended to meditate for 40 — 60 minutes (which was equivalent to the time of burning one stick of incense).

4.36 过午人事多扰，易落昏沉，然亦不必限定一炷香，只要诸缘放下，静坐片时，久久便有入头，不落昏沉睡着。

4.36 Normally, there would be distractions of worldly affairs after noon time. One would easily feel drowsy sitting for meditation. Hence, there would be no need to insist on a sitting of 40 — 60 minutes. One could simply relax and meditate for some moments. Over time, one would gain mastery to sit on a prolong basis, without feeling drowsy.

# Chapter 5: Light Reflex and Possible Mistakes and Deviations 第五章：回光差谬

5.1 吕祖曰："诸子工夫，渐渐纯熟，然枯木岩前错落多，正要细细开示。

5.1 Lü-zu continued: "Now as everyone gained mastery over the technique, I would like to caution that there would still be mistakes and pitfalls to avoid. Here, let me expound further.

5.2 此中消息，身到方知，吾今则可以言矣。

5.2 This information was appropriate at this stage, as matched by your personal experience in the practice.

5.3 吾宗与禅宗不同，有一步一步证验，请先言其差别处，然后再言证验。

5.3 Here, the difference between the Taoism and the Buddhist Zen practice was that in the "Dao" practice, there were clear milestones and confirmatory experiences every step of the way. First, I would explain the possible mistakes and deviations. In the next chapter, the milestones and confirmatory experiences would be discussed.

5.4 宗旨将行之际，予作方便，勿多用心，放教活泼泼地，令气和心适，然后入静。

5.4 Whenever one decided to practice this technique, some preparation would be necessary. Without any deliberate assertion, let the mind rest comfortably and the breath calm and steady. Under such ideal conditions, one began to meditate.

5.5 静时正要得机得窍，不可坐在无事中里，所谓无记空也。万缘放下之中，惺惺自若也。又不可以意兴承当，凡大认真，即易有此。非言不宜认真，但真消息，在若存若亡之间，以有意无意得之可也。惺惺不昧之中，放下自若也。又不可堕于蕴界，所谓蕴界者，乃五阴魔用事。

5.5 During meditation, the technique should be applied appropriately and intelligently. It should not be just mere sitting in "emptiness or void". As one relaxed, the mind should still stay alert, but not to the state of overly distracted. The requirement here would be for the mind to be kept adequately alert and serious, such that thoughts were let go naturally. But, one should not be too serious such that the mind could not relax. The wisdom here lied in the middle path between being and non-being, and between "thoughtfulness" and "thoughtlessness". A point to note during such state, one should be aware not to fall into the bondage of self-attachment.[19]

5.6 如一般入定，而槁木死灰之意多，大地阳春之意少。此则落于阴界，其炁冷，其息沉，且有许多寒衰景象，久之便堕木石。

5.6 In meditative state, if one experienced more "gloomy" thoughts (the text used "wood and ashes" to describe such thoughts) than "uplifting" thoughts (the text used "sunny

[19] The text here mentioned about the 5 accumulations or aggregates, a key tenet in Buddhist teaching, where the 5 aggregates of matter (physical sensory world), cognition, perception, feeling and reaction (collectively mind) created a delusional self identification that caused tremendous amount of attachment.

spring" to describe such thoughts), it meant that one had fallen into the "yin" realm with cold energy, heavy breath and decaying scenes. This would lead to becoming wood and stones if continued.

5.7 又不可随于万缘，如一入静，而无端众绪忽至，欲却之不能，随之反觉顺适，此名主为奴役，久之落于色欲界。上者生天，下者生狸奴中，若狐仙是也。

5.7 Another experience that one might have was the sudden influx of thoughts during meditation. While one's mind should not be led astray, one could not completely eradicate the thoughts either. As the result, one gave in and felt at ease by complying to these arising thoughts. This condition was as though the master had turned to be the slave of his own thoughts. As one carried on, it would lead to the realm of desire. In this regard, some would still ended up being born as human, while others might be born as an animal in the cat family, for instance as a fairy fox.

5.8 在名山中，亦自受用，风月花果，琪树瑶草，三五百年受用去，多至数千岁，然报尽还生诸趣中。

5.8 As a fairy fox, it would live in mountains, surrounded by abundant fruit trees, ample to sustain live up to three hundred to five hundred years, might be even more, up to a thousand years. At the end of life, it remained subjected to the wheel of Samsaric life[20], where it might be born again as human being.

5.9 此数者，皆差路也。差路既知，然后可求证验。"

---

20    Reincarnation and Karma put in a different way.

5.9 All the above were possible mistakes and deviations from the actual path. Having known this, one could now discuss about the milestones and confirmatory experiences.

# Chapter 6: Light Reflex and the Milestones and Confirmatory Experiences 第六章：回光证验[21]

6.1 吕祖曰："证验亦多，不可以小根小器承当，必思度尽众生。不可以轻心慢心承当，必须请事斯语。

6.1 According to Lü-zu, "There were many milestones and confirmatory experiences that one could witness personally during the light reflex practice. But it did not mean that one who achieved such state should get carried away with pride and tardiness. Instead, one should always keep an open mind and have the compassion to benefit all sentient beings.

6.2 静中绵绵无间，神情悦豫，如醉如浴，此为遍体阳和，金华乍吐也。

6.2 First, when entering the meditative state, one might continually feel at ease and immerse in joy. This was the early sign of the golden light ("jin hua, 金华") emerging, as explained in Chapter 1.

6.3 既而万籁俱寂，皓月中天，觉大地俱是光明境界，此为心体开明，金华正放也。

6.3 Subsequently, one would experience complete silence. One would also observe a full moon arising to reach the meridian passage, brightening up the earth. This was the

---

[21] In this chapter, the teacher explained two main milestones, each with three confirmatory experiences. Hence, the text is translated with this main structure in mind.

53

6.4 既而遍体充实，不畏风霜，人当之兴味索然者，我遇之精神更旺，黄金起屋，白玉为台；世间腐朽之物，我以真炁呵之立生；红血为乳，七尺肉团，无非金宝，此则金华大凝也。

6.4 Thirdly, one would experience a solid, healthy body, fully rejuvenated to face any hardship or challenge. Whilst others were uninspired, one would be in high spirit to face any challenge. It was like using gold to construct a house with white jade as support. One would protect all the worldly things that deteriorated, by breathing the energy of life (refer to Chapter 2) so that everything could come back to life immediately. The red blood served as the "milk" (the nutrients) for the precious seven-feet body structure. This was the sign of the golden light agglomerating.

6.5 第一段，是应《观无量寿经》云：日落大水，行树法象。

6.5 The three confirmatory experiences above marked the first main milestone for this practice. Achieving this first milestone would be similar to realizing the phenomenons as described in the ancient Buddhist text of "Amitāyurdhyāna-sūtra", namely sun meditation (first), water meditation (second) and tree meditation (fourth).[22]

6.6 日落者，从混沌立基，无极也。

6.6 In sun meditation, one realized the phenomenon of infinity (as explained in Chapter 2), through observing the

---

22  In Amitāyurdhyāna-sūtra, there are sixteen meditation stages. The three mentioned here are first, second and fourth on the list of sixteen (in bracket).

chaotic origination and formation of the universe.[23]

6.7 上善若水，清而无瑕，此即太极主宰，出震之帝也。

6.7 The Taoist founding master, Lao zi described water as having the supreme quality of purity and kindness. The water meditation further advanced the practice to grasp the phenomenon of supremacy ("太极", "tai ji").[24] From "tai ji,太极", the heaven and the earth came about, leading to the four elements of water, fire, wind and earth. The fifth chapter of "Yi Jing" (I Ching) recorded that the creation process as an explosion ("zhen").

6.8 震为木，故以行树象焉，七重行树，七窍光明也。

6.8 In I Ching, the explosion phenomenon belonged to the wood element. Hence, one progressed further with the tree meditation. In the "Amitāyurdhyāna-sūtra" text, it described the celestial trees, which represented the "brightening" of the seven orifices of the body.[25]

6.9 西北乾方，移一位为坎，日落大水，乾坎之象。坎为子方，冬至雷在地中，隐隐隆隆，至震而阳方出地上矣，行树之象

---

23  In Chinese philosophy, the chaos refers to the intertwining of the "yin" and "yang" (at state of infinity).
24  Here, the state of infinity above progresses to the state of supremacy after the creation of the universe. Here, I have used the word "supremacy" to translate the term "tai ji". After the creation, all phenomenons are ordered in some ways (i.e. "yin" and "yang" and others). Hence, a finite spectrum is present. Supremacy kind of reflect the very best within the spectrum, as oppose to infinity that occurs in a spectrum-less condition.
25  "Brightening" may not be the right word, the other closest translation is "enlightening" which is not quite right as well. Essentially, "七窍光明"colloquially means suddenly become bright, i.e. smart.

也，余可类推矣。

6.9 The three confirmatory experiences in the first milestone could be found in the I Ching context as well (by referring to the eight trigrams, "ba gua, 八卦"). The sun was found in the north west position, representing heaven ("qian, 乾"). The water, representing the moon, sat in the north position ("kan, 坎") and the tree's position was in the east ("zhen, 震"), represented by thunder.

6.10 第二段，即肇基于此，大地为冰，琉璃宝地，光明渐渐凝矣。所以有莲台而继之有佛也，金性即现，非佛而何，佛者大觉金仙也。

6.10 The second milestone would build upon the first milestone. As described in the "Amitāyurdhyāna-sūtra" text, one progressed from the sun and water meditation to the third stage of earth meditation. Here, one observed and realized the change phenomenon of the earth, being covered with snow and solidified into ice. The earth became transparent like glaze and light began to agglomerate. In subsequent meditation stages, one would advance to glimpse the Buddha's appearance (i.e. the second milestone). In this regard, the nature of golden light became fully visible. Wouldn't this be the Buddha? Thus, the practitioners who were fully realized in this technique, also reached Buddhahood.

6.11 此大段证验耳。现在证验，可考有三：一则坐去，神入谷中，闻人说话，如隔里许，一一明了，而声入皆如谷中答响，未尝不闻，我未尝一闻，此为神在谷中，随时可以自验；一则静中，目光腾腾，满前皆白，如在云中，开眼觅身，无从觅视，此为虚室生白，内外通明，吉祥止止也；一则静中，肉身絪缊，如绵如玉，坐中若留不住，而腾腾上浮，此为神归顶天，久之上升可以立待。

6.11 In order to witness the second milestone, one could experience three confirmatory signs. First, as one entered the meditative state, the spirit took hold. Here, one could hear and understand others clearly, but the sound seemed distant, echoing in the ears sense door. Next, being in meditative state, one's sight became dispersed. As though in the middle of cloud, one saw white all around. When one opened the eyes to look for his own body, one could not find it. It was an extremely auspicious sign to perceive such phenomenon. Third, one felt the generative force of one's body, like cotton and jade, during deep meditative state. One could no longer remain seated, and would feel floating upward. This marked the return of spirit to heaven. Over time, one could make the physical body float.

6.12 此三者，皆现在可验者也。然亦是说不尽的，随人根器，各现殊胜。

6.12 These three confirmatory experiences could be witnessed here and now. However, it would be impossible to explain every detail explicitly. Depending on one's spiritual talent, different confirmatory experiences could manifest.

6.13 如《止观》中所云：'善根发相是也。'此事如人饮水，冷暖自知，须自己信得过方真。

6.13 As described in the Buddhist book of contemplative meditation ("Zhi Guan Shu"), each practitioner would develop virtuosity differently. Like the temperature of water, only one who drank the water knew it. In a nutshell, one should practice to realize the milestones to be convinced of the technique.

6.14 先天一炁，即在现前证验中自讨，一炁若得，丹亦立成，此一粒真黍珠也。

6.14 One could obtain the energy of life (essence) [as in Chapter 2] from these confirmatory experiences. Once this was found, one could achieve immortality. This would be the genuine "yang" energy within the human body, in the form of corn-shape pearl.

6.15 一粒复一粒从微而至著。有时时之先天，一粒是也，有统体之先天，一粒乃至无量是也。一粒有一粒力量，此要自己胆大，为第一义。"

6.15 One would accumulate such "pearl" one at a time, in gradual phases ("pearl" by "pearl") or in entirety (from one "pearl" to uncountable "pearls"). Nevertheless, each "pearl" had its own power or strength. The main responsibility for the practitioner was to have strong determination in the practice.

# Chapter 7: Light Reflex and its Proactive Applications 第七章：回光活法

7.1 吕祖曰："回光循循然行去，不要废弃正业。

7.1 Lü-zu said, "This life reflex technique should be practised step by step, without affecting one's life proper.

7.2 古人云：'事来要应过，物来要识破。'

7.2 There was an ancient saying, "To cope with all matters that arose, to understand the real characteristics of all objects that came into possession."

7.3 子以正念治事，即光不为物转，光即自回。此时时无相之回光也，尚可行之，而况有真正著相回光乎？

7.3 If one lived life with right thought, the resultant light from this practice would not migrate to follow any external object. It would constantly remain in the state of light reflex.

7.4 日用间，能刻刻随事返照，不著一毫人我相。便是随地回光，此第一妙用

7.4 As part of the ordinary life, one should try to constantly self-reflect and contemplate rather than constantly comparing oneself with others. By doing so, one would constantly remain in the state of light reflex. This would be one of the proactive applications of this technique.

7.5 清晨能遣尽诸缘，静坐一、二时最妙。

59

7.5 In the morning, before all the distractions set in, one should ideally meditate for one to two hours. That would be most wonderful.

7.6 凡应事接物，只用返照法，便无一刻间断。如此行之，三月两月，天上诸真，必来印证矣。"

7.6 When handling any matters, one would constantly apply the reversal insights of the technique. Practising in this way persistently for two to three months, the saints and sages of the past would definitely notice the good effort and give the necessary approval.

# Chapter 8: The Virtuosity of Carefree Living
# 第八章：逍遥诀[26]

8.1 吕祖曰：

8.1 Lü-zu recited:

8.2 "玉清留下逍遥诀，四字凝神入炁穴。

8.2 "The "Dao" genesis deity (a key deity for Taoism, named "Yu Qing, 玉清") left this profound teaching of the virtuosity of carefree living; four words could describe the agglomeration of light, and the harnessing of the energy of life (essence).

8.3 六月俄看白雪飞，三更又见日轮赫。

8.3 Against the norm, one observed the sudden snow falling in June and bright sunlight shining at midnight.

8.4 水中吹起藉巽风，天上游归食坤德。

8.4 The wind blew amidst the water, whilst heaven returned to the receptive and nurturing earth.

8.5 更有一句玄中玄，无何有乡是真宅。'

---

[26] This is a summary chapter. The teacher kicked off with a four-sentence poem and the rest of the text explain each sentence in greater detail. Here, I have first translated the poem more literally following the four-sentence structure. Then, the details would follow with reference to each of the sentence.

8.5 There was one teaching even more profound, homeland in nowhere was the true residence."

8.6 律诗一首，玄奥已尽。

8.6 This poem fully explained the profound teaching of this technique.[27]

8.7 大道之要，不外无为而为四字。

8.7 To sum up, the essence of "dao" teaching could be found in the four words of "wu wei er wei, 无为而为", which literally means "non-action in action[28]" (i.e. letting things take their own course).

8.8 惟无为，故不滞方所形象，惟无为而为，故不堕顽空死虚。

8.8 One could break the bondage of any preconceived thought (or entanglement in forms and images) only by penetrating the ultimate reality (i.e. non-actionable state). Also, one could avoid falling into a nihilistic state only by accessing the ultimate reality (non-actionable state) in action.

8.9 作用不外一中，而枢机全在二目。

8.9 Here, the concept of "centrality / middle path" (an omnipresent phenomenon) worked its effect (see Chapter 3), placing the helm at the two eyes.

---

27   The explanation of the first sentence begins here.
28   In the west our similar colloquialism is: "let go, let god" (editor)

8.10 二目者，斗柄也，斡旋造化，转运阴阳，其大药则始终一水中金，即水乡铅而已。

8.10 The two eyes were like the "authority" that could mediate the universe of existence and rotate the "yin" and "yang'" energy. And the only remedy for immortality pointed to this same formula of golden light or ultimate vitality, as mentioned in the phrase "shui xiang qian, 水乡铅"of the ancient "Ru Yao Jing, 入药镜" text. (See Chapter 1.)

8.11 前言回光，乃指点初机，从外以制内，即辅以得主。此为中、下之士，修下二关，以透上一关者也。

8.11 Earlier, the light reflex technique was explained. Its instructions began with using external means to gain inner control, just like the king was aided by his courtiers. Such technique helped beginners to grasp the necessary foundation before advancing to higher levels.[29]

8.12 今头绪渐明，机括渐熟，天不爱道，直泄无上宗旨，诸子秘之秘之，勉之勉之！

8.12 Now, the understanding of the teaching has deepened. The grasping of the technique also improved. For the benefits of all beings, this supreme teaching was divulged. Hope all students would treasure it and practice it diligently.

---

29    For example, Chapter 3 expounded on placing the gazing of eyes at nose tip (external mean) to calm and concentration oneself (inner self), and Chapter 4 taught about using breathing (external mean) to calm the mind (internal).

8.13 夫回光其总名耳。工夫进一层，则光华盛一番，回法更妙一番。

8.13. Here, "light reflex" was the term used to describe the overall technique. As one progressed, the golden light perceived would be more and more magnificent. The state of light reflex would also become more and more wonderful.

8.14 前者由外制内，今则居中御外。前者即辅相主，今则奉主宣猷，面目一大颠倒矣。

8.14 In the beginning, one applied certain external tools to gain inner control (like the king being aided by the courtiers). Now, one could reign inside to rule the external surrounding (the king was now in the position to give command). A complete reversal of roles would occur.

8.15 法子欲入静，先调摄身心，自在安和，放下万缘，一丝不挂。

8.16 One of the requirements of this technique was fine-tuning the body and mind as one entered into meditative state. One should be calm and at ease, leaving behind all worldly desires and affairs.

8.16 天心正位乎中，然后两目垂帘，如奉圣旨，以召大臣，孰敢不遵。

8.16 Bringing one's awareness to the third eye, one would lower the eye lids to half-close position. This was as though one had received an edict from the king. No one dares not to obey.

8.17 次以二目内照坎宫，光华所到，真阳即出以应之。

8.17 Then, one would start by focusing the eyes' vision inward at the head area. [30] Wherever the golden light permeated, it would be met with the true "yang" energy.

8.18 离外阳而内阴，乾体也。一阴入内而为主，随物生心，顺出流转，

8.18 In the I Ching, 8th trigrams, the "li" trigram had the quality of "yang" externally and "yin" internally. In its original form, it carried the "yang" quality of the "qian" trigram. However, a "yin" element intruded and took charge, thus one became desirous of worldly thoughts and external matters.[31]

8.19 今回光内照，不随物生，阴气即住，而光华注照，则纯阳也。

8.19 Now, with the attainment of light reflex, one would no longer be subjected to the worldly desires, where the "yin" energy was tamed and reigned in. At the same time, the golden light shone through, dispelling all "yin" energy to put one in the state of pure "yang" condition.

8.20 同类必亲，故坎阳上腾，非坎阳也，仍是乾阳应乾阳耳。

8.20 In this regard, the "yang" condition would start to attract similar kind of energy. Hence, the "yang" energy

---

30  From various Chinese text, "坎宫kan gong" refers to the north position. Here, I have directly pointed to the head area...
31  This is consistent with Chapter 2 which described the wondering spirit leading one to roll unceasingly from life to life.

in the "kan" trigram would increase many folds. Not only the "yang" energy referred here belonged to the "kan" trigram, it was the same "yang" energy as in the "qian" trigram as well.

8.21 二物一遇，便纽结不散，絪缊活动，倏来倏去，倏浮倏沉，自己元宫中，恍若太虚无量，遍身轻妙欲腾，所谓云满千山也。

8.21 Once the two "yang" energies met, they intertwined intimately, allowing for generative forces to take effect, suddenly arising and passing away and suddenly floating and sinking away. Here, one would feel the extreme vastness and lightness of the body (from the throat area to the abdomen area, as though one would float upward (See Chapter 6)). This was described metaphorically as the state of being surrounded by cloud amidst the thousand mountains.

8.22 次则来往无踪，浮沉无辨，脉住炁停，此则真交媾矣，所谓月涵万水也。

8.22 Then, one progressed further where the arising and passing away disappeared without any trace and the floating and sinking away diminished without any discernment. Suddenly, the pulse and breath would stop. This was referred to as the state of true union of the energy of life between the "kan" and "li" phenomenons. The metaphoric description of this state was the moon encompassing all waters.

8.23 俟其冥冥中，忽然天心一动，此则一阳来复，活子时也。

8.23 Waiting patiently in this state, the third eye might move suddenly (also referred to Chapter 2). This signified the recovery of the live "yang" energy, energizing one's life.

8.24 然而此中消息要细说，凡人一视一听，耳目逐物而动，物去则已，此之动静，全是民庶，而天君反随之役，是尝与鬼居矣。

8.24 However, further explanation was needed to describe this state in detail. Mere mortal used eyes and ears sense doors to see and hear. The two sense doors restlessly followed the external objects all the time, as though the people / citizens were all carrying out their daily activities, without obeying the king. Worse still, the king joined to serve the citizens instead. This was no different from living with a ghost within.

8.25 今则一动一静，皆与人居，天君乃真人也。

8.25 Now, the practitioner could leave the ghost behind, to be with the "human" instead. [32]

8.26 彼动即与之俱动，动则天根；静则与之俱静，静则月窟；静动无端，亦与之为静动无端；休息上下，亦与之为休息上下，所谓天根月窟闲来往也。

8.26 Further, as and when the king moved[33] in tandem with the people / citizens, such movement was termed "tian gen" (天根). Oppositely, as and when the king became silent with the people / citizens following suit, such silence

---

32  "Human" here is meant the real enlightened being within oneself.
33  Became active.

was termed "yue ku" (月窟). Following this, the king might become active or silent purposelessly, and the people / citizens would follow suit as well. Once the king rested completely, the people / citizens would rest too. This was termed the idling between the "tian gen" and "yue ku".

8.27 天心镇静，动违其时，则失之嫩；天心已动，而后动以应之，则失之老；天心一动，即以真意上升乾宫，而神光视顶，为导引焉，此动而应时者也。

8.27 If the third eye was calmed, moving it would be premature. Once the third eye had moved, tracking it from behind would be overly mature (too late). The right way should be that once the third eye moved, one would bring the mind awareness to the top of the head. The gaze of the eyes also fixated upward as the leading guide.

8.28 天心既升乾顶，游扬自得，忽而欲寂，急以真意引入黄庭，而目光视中黄神室焉，既而欲寂者，一念不生矣。

8.28 When the attention moved from the third eye to the top of the head, and while moving freely, it stopped suddenly. One should quickly apply the mind awareness again to bring the attention to the chest area (middle "dan tian"). Similarly, the gaze of the eyes also be fixated in the same mid section. Continuing in this manner, one achieved the state of thoughtlessness.

8.29 视内者，忽忘其视矣，尔时身心，便当一场大放，万缘泯迹，即我之神室炉鼎，亦不知在何所，欲觅己身，了不可得，此为天入地中，众妙归根之时也，即此便是凝神入炁穴。

8.29 For self-observation practitioner, the body and mind could be free from all desirous entanglements as one forget his gaze, reaching the state of thoughtlessness, such that one no longer knew where the area of attention was (neither the chest area (middle "dan tian") nor the abdomen area (lower "dan tian")), not even one's body. This state was termed "tian ru di zhong" (天入地中), meaning literally that the heaven penetrated into the earth. This was the moment where all returned to its respective roots, i.e. the agglomerated spirit entering into the energy channels (essence).

8.30 夫一回光也，始而散者欲敛，六用不行，此为涵养本原，添油接命也。既而敛者，自然优游，不费纤毫之力，此为安神祖窍，翕聚先天也。既而影响俱灭，寂然大定，此为蛰藏炁穴，众妙归根也。

8.30 Accordingly, one could apply the light reflex technique to realize the various milestones and confirmatory experiences. In the beginning, the "light" was dispersed and scattered. Later, one improved by being more and more restrained but focused. All the six senses (eyes, ears, nose, mouth, body and mind) no longer worked. This was termed "the restraint of one's origin, adding oil to fuel one's life" (hereafter: the restraint state). [literal translation of 涵养本源，添油接命] Next, one who managed to restrain but focus on the "light" could move the attention / awareness freely and effortlessly. This was termed "the state of achieving spiritual peace, gathering the energy of life (essence)" (hereafter: the peace state). [literal translation of 安神祖窍，翕聚先天] Then, one entered into the state of firm stillness, unperturbed by any thought or worldly entanglement. This was termed "the hibernation of the energy channels (essence) as though all were returning to its respective roots" (hereafter: the hibernation state). [literal translation of 蛰藏气穴，众妙归根][34]

8.31 一节中具有三节，一节中具有九节，俱是后日发挥。

8.31 In this regard, the technique comprised one main instruction, broken into three sub-sections. In fact, the main instruction could be further divided into nine sub-sections. Detail to be explained and expounded later.

8.32 今以一节中，具三节言之，当其涵养而初静也。翕聚亦为涵养，蛰藏亦为涵养，至后而涵养皆蛰藏矣。中一层可类推，不易处而处分矣，此为无形之窍，千处万处一处也。

8.32 Now, let us focused on this concept of the main instruction being divided into three sub-sections. At the initial meditative stage, one experienced the restraint state. Here, both the peace state and the hibernation state were essentially the same as the restraint state. Similarly, as one reached the peace state, both the restraint state and the hibernation state were the same as the peace state. Lastly, one achieved the hibernation state, which was similar to both the restraint state and the peace state. One's attention / awareness could remain but these different states would manifest themselves naturally. This was described as the "formless orifice". The numerous points of attention were all only one point of attention.

8.33 不易时而时分焉，此为无候之时。元会运世一刻也。

8.33 Just like time, it remained as was but would divide

---

[34] Here, the teacher made reference to the ancient Taoism text, "Xing Ming Gui Zhi, 性命圭旨", believed to be written by one of the main disciples of "Guan Yin Zi" (Chapter 3).

itself naturally. This was described as the "timeless time". The various divisions of time were all only one moment of time.

8.34 凡心非静极，则不能动，动动忘动，非本体之动也。

8.34 Generally, the desirous heart would only remain still unless one reached an extremely calm state in meditation. In fact, the desirous heart would move restlessly all the time.

8.35 故曰感于物而动，性之欲也，若不感于物而动，即天之动也。是知以物而动，性之欲也，若不以物而自动，即天之动也。

8.35 Therefore, if the heart was entangled by worldly feelings and thoughts, it was driven by human desires. If the heart no longer entangled by the worldly feelings and thoughts, it was driven by the universe (or the ultimate truth).

8.36 不以天之动对天之性，句落下说个欲字，欲在有物也，此为出位之思，动而有动矣。

8.36 The word "desire" (Chinese character: 欲 ("yu")) hinged upon external objects. One should not equate the act of the universe to the nature of the universe. Here, the underlying thought was beyond the norm, acting within the act.

8.37 一念不起，则正念乃生，此为真意。

8.37 If one could achieve thoughtlessness, the "right thought" [as similar to samma sankappa, one of the eightfold noble paths in the Buddhist doctrine] would arise. Here, the "right thought" was equivalent to the "true mind".

8.38 寂然大定中，而天机忽动，非无意之动乎？无为而为，即此意也。

8.38 When one was firmly in still meditative state, wouldn't any sudden act be act in thoughtlessness? This was the real meaning of the aforementioned "non-action in action" (i.e. letting thing take its own course).

8.39 诗首二句，全括金华作用。

8.39 Now, referring to the poem at the beginning of this chapter, these first two verses fully described the efficacy of the golden light / flower technique.

8.40 次二句是日月互体意，六月即离火也，白雪飞即离中真阴将返乎坤也。三更即坎水也，目轮即坎中一阳将赫然而返乎乾也。取坎填离，即在其中。

8.40 The next two verses meant to describe the phenomenon of the sun-moon exchange. Here, June referred to the south pole position (i.e. the "li" trigram) with the fire element. The snowfall represented the real "yin" energy, returning to the south west position (i.e. the "kun" trigram, the receptive earth). In contrast, the midnight reference represented the north pole position (i.e. the "kan" trigram) with the water element. The sunlight meant the real "yang" energy, returning to the north west position (i.e. the "qian: trigram). To summarize, these two verses described the phenomenon of "withdrawing from "kan" and filling into "li".

8.41 次二句说斗柄作用，升降全机，水中非坎乎。目为巽风，目光照入坎宫，摄召太阳之精是也。天上即乾宫，游归食坤德，即神入炁中，天入地中，养火也。

8.41 The fifth and sixth verses talked about the function of the "authority" that could control the entire energy channel (essence). The water here referred to the water element in the "kan" trigram, whereas the wind essentially meant the eyes. As the eyes were fixated in the north pole position (top of the head), all the essence of the sun ("yang" energy) was summoned and garnered. As the heaven returned to the nurturing and receptive earth, this precisely described the state where the agglomerated spirit entered into the energy channel (essence).[35]

8.42 末二句是指诀中之诀，诀中之诀，始终离不得，所谓洗心涤虑，为沐浴也。圣学以知止始，以止至善终，始乎无极，归乎无极。佛以无住而生心，为一大藏教旨。吾道以'致虚'二字，完性命全功。

8.42 Lastly, the final two verses were the most profound, which essentially led the practitioner to undertake purification of the mind (i.e. the "mind bath"). Confucius, in essence, taught about this similar process where one would begin to "stop all knowing", till one reached the final point of ultimate kindness (i.e. one began with the state of infinity and ended with the state of infinity as well). Buddha (in particular the Varjayana practice) also taught about the arising of the free heart / mind, without any "home" entrapment. In Taoism, the aim of life was to reach

---

35   This was mentioned earlier, repeated here.

the state of ultimate truth.

8.43 总之三教不过一句，为出死入生之神丹。

8.43 In conclusion, all the three teachings (Confucius, Buddhism and Taoism) could be summarized in one sentence — the ultimate aim was to achieve the elixir of life, breaking away from the bondage of life and death.

8.44 '神丹'为何？曰一切处无心而已。吾道最秘者沐浴，如此一部全功，不过'心空'二字，足以了之，今一言指破，省却数十年参访矣。

8.44 What was the elixir of life? It referred to the unhindered heart / mind that was constantly in the state of "nothingness". Though the "mind bath" was the best kept secret of Taoism, the main tenets of this teaching / technique lied in the concept of the heart / mind of "emptiness". Now, with this principle revealed, one could save tens of years of contemplation.

8.45 子辈不明一节中具三节，我以佛家'空、假、中'三观为喻，三观先空，看一切物皆空；次假，虽知其空，然不毁万物，仍于空中建立一切事；既不毁万物，而又不著万物，此为中观。

8.45 For those who were still unclear about the concept of the main instruction being divided into three subsections (as expounded earlier), I would explain further using the Buddha's teaching of "emptiness, delusion and centrality / middle path". For the Buddhist practitioner, the contemplative meditation began with "emptiness". Here, one penetrated to realize the truth of all minds and matters, which were "empty" in nature. This was followed by contemplating the second truth of "delusion". Though one realized the "emptiness" nature of all phenomenons, one lived in the delusional "apparent truth", where all worldly things were built upon and seemed indestructible. As one gained the wisdom of "emptiness" and "delusion", one could penetrate the third truth of the "middle path".

8.46 当其修空观时，亦知万物不可毁，而又不著，此兼三观也。然毕竟以看得空为得力，故修空观。则空固空，假亦空，中亦空。

8.46 As one meditated on "emptiness", one would also realize the "delusion" of all the worldly things that seemed indestructible. Hence, one would develop the right understanding of non-attachment. In this regard, one practised all three teachings concurrently. Nevertheless, one anchored the practice via the "emptiness" contemplation. Therefore, it was said that "emptiness" meditation was similar to both the "delusion" meditation and the "middle path" meditation.

8.47 修假观，是用上得力居多，则假固假，空亦假，中亦假。

8.47. Following the same train of thought, for those who anchored their practice via the "delusion" contemplation, it was said that the "delusion" meditation was no different from the "emptiness" meditation and the "middle path" meditation.

8.48 中道时亦作空想，然不名为空而名为中矣。亦作假观，然不名为假而名为中矣，至于中则不必言矣。

8.48 Again, the same deduction applied for those practitioners who anchored their practice via the "middle path" contemplation. During the "middle path" meditation, one realized the truth of emptiness. Instead of calling it "empty" in nature, one called it the "middle path". Also, one would realized the truth of delusion. Instead of calling it "delusional" in nature, one called it the "middle path".

8.49 吾虽有时单言离，有时兼说坎，究竟不曾移动一句。

8.49 Sometimes, I would refer singly to the "li" trigram, or to both the "li" and "kan" trigrams concurrently. But, the actual meaning remained unchanged.

8.50 开口提示：枢机全在二目。

8.50 In the beginning of this chapter, I highlighted on the importance of the two eyes, holding the helm.

8.51 所谓枢机者用也，用即斡旋造化，非言造化止此也。六根七窍，悉是光明藏，岂取二目，而他概不问乎，用坎阳，仍用离光照摄，即此便明。

8.51 The helm here meant any tool used for mediating the nature (i.e. the universe of existence) to bring to life all existence (as opposed to terminating / confining it). All together, human had six sense doors (eyes, ears, nose, mouth / tongue, body and mind) and seven apertures / orifices (eyes (two), ears (two), nose (two and mouth (one)). All were equally important leading to the noble path.[36] While the importance of the two eyes was emphasized, it did not mean that these other senses and orifices should be

---

36   a concept in the Buddhist doctrine

ignored. In the same way, not only one applied the "yang" energy in the "kan" trigram, one would make use of the light referred to in the "li" trigram as well.

8.52 朱子云阳师讳元育，尝云：'瞎子不好修道，聋子不妨。'与吾言暗合，特表其主辅轻重耳。

8.52 The renown teacher, Zhu Yuan Yu (朱元育)[37] once taught that, "It was more difficult for the blind to practice "dao", as compared to the deaf." This was no different from my emphasis on the two eyes. Here, my aim was simply to differentiate the main tool from the supporting tools.

8.53 日月原是一物，其日中之暗处，是真月之精，月窟不在月而在日，所谓月之窟也，不然自言月足矣。月中之白处，是真日之光，日光反在月中，所谓天之根也，不然自言天足矣。

8.53 Going back to the sun-moon exchange, both the sun and moon referred here were essentially the same thing. When the sun was in complete darkness, it was effectively the moon. Thus, "yue ku" (mentioned earlier in the example of the relationship between the king and the people / citizens, meaning literally the hole (ku, 窟) in moon (yue, 月)) was not on the moon but on the sun instead. "Yue ku" meant the "hole" left by the moon on the sun. Otherwise, one could just refer to the moon as was. Similarly, when the moon was in complete brightness, it was effectively the sun. The moon fully reflected the sunlight. Thus, "tian gen" (literal meaning the root (gen, 根) of heaven (tian, 天)) in the same example referred to this same phenomenon. Otherwise, one could just refer to

---

[37] very little background available

the heaven as was. There was no need to add the root part.

8.54 一日一月，分开止是半个，合来方成一个全体。如一夫一妇，独居不成室家，有夫有妇，方算得一家完全。

8.54 Further, when the sun and the moon were separated, only half the globe could be seen. If combined, the whole globe could be seen. Just like the example of husband and wife, if separated in solitude, there was effectively no marriage. Only when the husband and wife were together, the marriage was considered whole / complete.

8.55 然而物难喻道，夫妇分开，不失为两人，日月分开，不成全体矣。知此则耳目犹是也。

8.55 However, this worldly example of marriage between husband and wife was not entirely appropriate. When both the husband and the wife separated, they were still two individuals on their own. Separating the sun and the moon in this case, the wholeness could not be perceived any more. This was precisely how one could understand the use of the eyes and the ears, both made up the entirety.

8.56 吾谓瞎子已无耳，聋子已无目，如此看来，说甚一物，说甚两目，说甚六根，六根一根也。

8.56 Therefore, when I said that the blind had no ear and the deaf had no eye, my real meaning was not referring to any one particular sense door but in fact, all the six senses were effectively one.

8.57 说甚七窍，七窍一窍也。

8.57 Similarly, all the seven orifices were effectively one as well.

8.58 吾言只透露其相通处，所以不见有两，子辈专执其隔处，所以随处换却眼睛。"

8.58 All my explanation above aimed to bring out the commonality of the senses and the orifices. In practice, they were seen as the same thing. Hence, one could switch the attention from the eyes as wished.

# Chapter 9: Building Foundation in One Hundred Days 第九章：百日筑基

9.1 吕祖曰："《心印经》云：'回风混合，百日功灵。'

9.1 Lü-zu said, "In the ancient Buddhist text "Xin Yin Jing" (see Chapter 1), it was taught that by applying the technique of "wind reversal and combination" [Literal translation: 回 (reversal) 风 (wind) 混合 (combination)], one could achieve the elixir of life in one hundred days."

9.2 总之立基百日，方有真光如。

9.2 In short, one would practice at least one hundred days to lay a strong foundation, in order to realize the ultimate truth (or at least to derive the benefits of the practice).

9.3 子辈尚是目光，非神火也，非性光也，非慧智炬烛也。

9.3 In the beginning, the light reflex that one achieved was merely an eye sight perception. It was neither the light of spirit, nature nor wisdom.

9.4 回之百日，则精炁自足，真阳自生，水中自有真火，以此持行，自然交媾，自然结胎，吾方在不识不知之天，而婴儿自成矣。若略作意见，便是外道。

9.4 When one performed the light reflex for one hundred days, both the essence and the energy of life became abundant (see Chapter 2). Pure "yang" energy would naturally arise (i.e. within the essence of the body (water), spirit (fire)). If one practised persistently, the benefits would

81

result naturally, leading to the inception of a noble being (see Chapter 2). While one might be ignorant and unable to understand everything, the embryo had developed and grown naturally (see Chapter 3). Conversely, if one applied thoughts / consciousness deliberately, the results / benefits might allude oneself.

9.5 百日立基，非百日也。一日立基，非一日也。一息立基，非呼吸之谓也。

9.5 However, the one hundred days duration was not a hard requirement. Just like when one mentioned about building foundation in one day, it did not necessarily mean one day only. Similarly, when one mentioned about building foundation in one breath, it did not necessarily mean one breath only.

9.6 息者自心也，自心为息，元神也，元炁也，元精也。升降离合，悉从心起，有无虚实，咸在念中。

9.6 The Chinese had an old saying that the breath was the reflection of one's heart / mind (see Chapter 4). Pictorially, the Chinese character of breath (息) was made up by combining two Chinese characters of self (自) and heart / mind (心). How the primordial spirit, the energy of life and the essence interacted within self depended entirely on the heart / mind, resulting in all thoughts / consciousness (tangible or intangible, real or unreal).

9.7 一息一生持，何止百日，然百日亦一息也。

9.7 There was a saying, "A breath kept for life." Here, the duration was more than one hundred days. Nevertheless, one should understand that even over the one hundred days duration, a breath was merely a breath.

9.8 百日只在得力，昼间得力，夜中受用，夜中得力，昼间受用。

9.8 The key element within the one hundred days foundation period was the quality of the practice. If one practised effectively in the day time, one could benefit at once by night time. If one practised effectively in the night time, one could benefit at once by day time.

9.9 百日立基，玉旨耳。

9.9 The concept of building foundation in one hundred days was introduced (or as instructed) by the Jade Emperor.[38]

9.10 上真言语，无不与人身应。真师言语，无不与学人应。

9.10 All the sayings and teachings by the heavenly beings could benefit us directly, as human beings. All the sayings and teachings by the enlightened ones could benefit us directly, as the "dao" practitioners.

9.11 此是玄中玄，不可解者也。

9.11 This was the profound truth that was not easily comprehensible.

9.12 见性乃知，所以学人，必求真师授记，任性发出，——

---

38   Ruler of heaven and all realms of existence, as believed in Chinese folklore and Taoist mythology.

皆验。"

9.12 Only when the practitioner penetrated the profound truth of the ultimate reality, can this be understood thoroughly. When one received the truth teaching from the enlightened one, any part of the teaching could be realized and could yield immediate benefits.

# Chapter 10: Light of Nature (Cognition), Light of Consciousness (Recognition) 第十章：性光、识光

10.1 吕祖曰："回光之法，原通行住坐卧，只要自得机窍。

10.1 Lü-zu taught: "The light reflex practice could be carried out in any position, sitting, standing, walking or laying down, so long as one mastered the key essence of the teaching and technique.

10.2 吾前开示云：'虚室生白'，光非白邪。

10.2 Earlier, I mentioned about witnessing the confirmatory sign where one's sight became dispersed as though in the middle of the cloud, seeing white all around (see Chapter 6). This, however, did not mean that the light was white in colour.

10.3 但有一说，初未见光时，此为效验，若见为光，而有意著之，即落意识，非性光也。

10.3 One reminder for all of you. If, during practice, without seeing any light, such experience of seeing white all around would indeed be considered the confirmatory sign of the practice. If, however, one saw light and attached consciousness to it, such experience would not count as the confirmatory progress because one was still in the realm of consciousness (apparent world). Such light was not the light of nature as existed in the ultimate realm.

10.4 子不管他有光无光，只要无念生念。

10.4 Therefore, one need not bother if there was light or not. The key was to ensure that one reached the state of thoughtlessness and the arising of right thought (see Chapter 8).

10.5 何为无念？千休千处得；何为生念？一念一生持，此念乃正念，与平日念不同。

10.5 What was the state of thoughtlessness? It referred to the state of practising / meditating any time, anywhere (in the Buddhist doctrine). What was the arising of right thought? It referred to the state of one thought kept for life (also in the Buddhist doctrine). Here, the thought that arose were different from the everyday worldly thoughts. The thoughts that arose had the quality of right thought (as in the eightfold noble path of the Buddhist doctrine).

10.6 今心为念，念者现在心也。

10.6 Pictorially, the Chinese character of thought (念) was the combination of two Chinese characters — now (今) and heart / mind (心). The arising of right thought referred to this heart / mind of the present.

10.7 此心即光即药。

10.7 Such heart / mind was essentially both the light (for enlightenment) and the medicine (for curing the malice / sickness of life).

10.8 凡人视物，任眼一照去，不及分别，此为'性光'，如镜之无心而照也，如水之无心而鉴也。

10.8 Under normal circumstances. When human being first got in contact with the external matters, it would merely cognize the matter without any evaluation. This was referred to as the "cognition" phase. It merely cognized the matter, just like the mirror and still water reflecting their objects as were.[39]

10.9 少刻即为'识光'，以其分别也。镜有影已无镜矣，水有象已无水矣。光有识尚何光哉

10.9 From the "cognition" phase, one moved to the "recognition" phase, where the mind would give evaluation. Once there was reflection in the mirror or in the still water, the mirror and the still water were no longer mere mirror or still water. Similarly, light with consciousness was not the light that this technique was after.

10.10 子辈初则'性光'，转念则识，识起而光杳无可觅，非无光也，光已为识矣。

10.10 As one's cognition turned to become recognition, this was similar to attaching consciousness to the light, as such the light of nature was gone without a trace, could not be found. It did not mean that there was no light, but

---

39　The term used here (cognize, cognition) is reference against the five aggregates of the Buddhist teaching – matter (one) plus mind (four). The four mind aggregates are cognition (vinnana), recognition and evaluation (sanna), feeling (vedana) and reaction (sankhara). In the Buddhist doctrine, the five aggregates make up an individual (self). In the apparent world, there is a lot of attachment to this self, creating afflictions such as greed, anger, jealousy, etc., resulting in unceasing suffering.

the light had become attached to consciousness.

10.11 黄帝曰：'声动不生声而生响'，即此义也。

10.11 Huang Di (The Yellow Emperor, regarded as the initiator of the Chinese civilization) once said, "Sounding without sound was the loudest." - Metaphor that hints the phenomenon of the light.

10.12 《楞严推勘入门》曰：'不在尘，不在识，惟选根'，此则何意？

10.12 The ancient Buddhist text "Leng Yan Tui Kan Ru Men stated that "Not in "dust", not in consciousness, but only in the "root"." What did this mean?

10.13 尘是外物，所谓器界也。与吾了不相涉，逐之则认物为己。

10.13 Here, "dust" referred to the matter aggregate. In Buddhism, this was the realm of apparent world. It supposedly had no self (or an independent core). However, when the heart / mind (i.e. consciousness in other word) became attached to it, one would identify the object as "I am", "mine" or "myself".

10.14 物必有还，通还户牖，明还日月，借他为自，终非吾有。

10.14. The very nature of all matters was such that they owed their existence to some other matters / circumstances as well. For instance, the very nature / function of window was enabling air to flow between indoor and outdoor. However, without air flow, the window lost its function, and vice versa, without the window, the air could not flow. Both were dependent of each other. Similarly, the very nature / function of the sun and moon was to shine light. Both the light and the sun and moon were dependent on each other. Even if one insisted on claiming ownership of the dependent object, the dependent object would eventually still not belong to one another.

10.15 至于不汝还者，非汝而谁。

10.15 Based on this dependency theory, once one reached the core nature which could not be attributed to others nor dependent on others for its existence, such core would be nothing but the "true self" (i.e. the essence).

10.16 明还日月，见日月之明无还也。

10.16 Referring back to the sun and moon example, when one perceived the sun and moon shining light. This ought to be an irreversible mental imprint in one's mind.

10.17 天有无日月之时，人无有无见日月之性。若然则分别日月者，还可与为吾有耶。

10.17 In reality, there were times where the sun and moon were hidden from the sky and darkness reigned. But, the human mind continued to have the thought of the sun and moon shining light (and became attached to such view, failing to realize the true reality of dependency between the sun and moon and light).

10.18 不知因明暗而分别者，当明暗两忘之时，分别何在，故亦有还，此为内尘也。

10.18 Without understanding the reality as it was, one would differentiate between brightness and darkness. Penetrating into the ultimate truth, both were in actual fact no different from one another. However, there would still be remnant of mental imprint within oneself. This was called the "internal dust" (literal translation of 内尘), i.e. internal afflictions or mental hindrances.

10.19 惟见性无还，见见之时，见非是见，则见性亦还矣。

10.19 Only when the practitioner penetrated the profound truth of the ultimate reality can all the dependencies be broken. Again, at such state of penetration, one saw the truth without actually seeing the truth, as even the dependency of seeing the truth was broken.

10.20 还者还其识念流转之见性，即阿难使汝流转，心目为咎也。

10.20 Such truth penetration was the state of "filtering" out all recognitions and thoughts. In the ancient Buddhist text of "Leng Yan Jing" (Tang Dynasty, 705 A.C., quoted in Chapter 1 before), similar teaching was recorded as Buddha Sakyamuni explained to his personal attendant cum disciple, Ananda, that one rolled unceasingly in the apparent world because of the hindered or obscured mind.

10.21 初入还辨见时，上七者，皆明其一一有还，故留见性，以为阿难拄杖。究竟见性既带八识（眼识、耳识、鼻识、舌识、身识、意识、传送识、阿赖耶识），非真不还也。

10.21 Buddha Sakyamuni continued explaining that as

one penetrated the truth about the dependency theory, one could penetrate the truth of dependency for seven out of eight consciousnesses. [The Eight Consciousnesses is a classification developed in the tradition of the Yogacara school of Buddhism. They enumerate the five senses, supplemented by the mind, the "obscuration" of the mind (manas), and finally the fundamental store-house consciousness (alaya), which is the basis of the other seven.] Here, the eighth consciousness of alaya consciousness was left not penetrated just as yet for Ananda's case. [Ananda was Buddha Sakyamuni's personal attendant cum disciple. He did not gain enlightenment (reaching arahat-hood), as many other Buddha's disciples did, until the passing away of Buddha Sakyamuni.] In any case, the entire truth penetration process would include all the eight consciousnesses (eyes, ears, nose, tongue, body, mind, manas and alaya).

# Chapter 11: The Exchange Between the "yin" and "yang" Energy 第十一章：坎离交媾[40]

11.1 吕祖曰："凡漏泄精神，动而交物者，皆离也。凡收转神识，静而中涵者，皆坎也。

11.1 Lü-zu continued his teaching, "The "li" trigram pointed to any phenomenon leading to leakage of the essence and spirit, causing us to become attached to external matters / objects. In the opposite manner, the "kan" trigram referred to any phenomenon leading to accumulation of spirit and consciousness, causing us to become equanimous and restrained in the middle path.

11.2 七窍之外走者为离，七窍之内返者为坎。

11.2 In other words, when the seven orifices seek external objects, it was the "li" phenomenon whereas when the seven orifices reversed inward, it was the "kan" phenomenon.

11.3 一阴主于逐色随声，一阳主于返闻收见。

11.3 Another characteristic of the "li" phenomenon related to the "yin" energy of focusing on external sights and sounds. As for the "yang" energy within the "kan" phenomenon, the focus was more to internalize the sights and sounds.

11.4 坎离即阴阳，阴阳即性命，性命即身心，身心即神炁。

---
40 The interplay between the "kan" and "li" trigrams / phenomenons.

11.4 Therefore, both the "kan" and "li" trigrams were "yin" and "yang" representations respectively, and "yin" and "yang" were effectively life. Here, life meant the body and mind, and the body and mind referred to the spirit and energy of life.

11.5 一自敛息精神，不为境缘流转，那是真交。而沉默趺坐时，又无论矣。"

11.5 Once the practitioner began to subdue the breath, one's essence and spirit would be preserved, unaffected by the external matters and environments. Having accomplished this, one had, in fact, achieved the "real" exchange of the "kan" and "li" phenomenons. More so, if one was able to keep still and calm to sit for meditation.

# Chapter 12: The Circulation of Energy 第十二章：周天[41]

12.1 吕祖曰："周天非以气作主，以心到为妙诀。

12.1 Lü-zu continued, "The actual definition of "zhou tian, 周天"(hereafter: circulation of energy) is not energy-based, but mind-based."

12.2 若毕竟如何周天，是助长也，无心而守，无意而行。

12.2 If one asked how should the energy cycle be executed, it would be as though one tried to pull up the seedling to help it grow (i.e. unnecessary action that could make matter worse). The energy cycle was a natural phenomenon, not to be pursued. One should just maintain the awareness without conscious mindfulness and practice without deliberate thoughtfulness.

12.3 仰观乎天，三百六十五度，刻刻变迁，而斗柄终古不动，吾心亦犹是也。

12.3 When we looked up the sky (into space), the firmament was divided into 360º, constantly in motion (i.e.

---

41 Several possible translations could be used here. First, "周天"refer to a circle with 360 degree (º). It also carries the meaning of the universe. More specifically in Taoism / "Qigong", "周天" is commonly used as a technical term to refer to the full circulation of the energy in the body. In this regard, there are mainly two types of energy cycle — "small" energy cycle (refers to the energy circulation within a certain section of the body), and "big" energy cycle (refers to the energy circulation of the entire body as well as the energy circulation and exchange between the body and the universe).

rotating on its own axis and orbiting around the sun). But, one could notice an "anchor" in the sky (i.e. the Polaris or the North Star) which remained motionless while the stars rotated around it. Our heart / mind acted in the same way.

12.4 心即璇玑，炁即众星。

12.4 Our heart / mind was just like the "anchor", whilst the energy was like the stars rotating around it.

12.5 吾身之炁，四肢百体，原是贯通，不要十分着力。

12.5 The energy in our body by nature perforated throughout our entire body structure. Hence, one need not exert oneself during the practice.

12.6 于此锻炼识神，斩除妄见，然后药生，药非有形之物，此性光也。而即先天之真炁，然必于大定后方见，并无采法，言采者大谬矣。

12.6 The focus should be placed to train the consciousness such that one could eliminate all the wrong views, leading to the emergence of the medicine (cure) of life. The "medicine" here was not something tangible, but was essentially the light of nature (i.e. mere cognition), which was the energy of life. One could obtain such "medicine" only in deep meditative state. There was no such thing as "harvesting the medicine". Anyone who talked about "harvesting the medicine" was not on the right path.

12.7 见之既久，心地光明，自然心空漏尽，解脱尘海。

12.7 As time passed, the practitioner who was able to

maintain such energy of life would gradually purify the mind, liberating oneself from the shackle of samsaric life and death.

12.8 若今日龙虎，明日水火，终成妄想。吾昔受火龙真人口诀如是，不知丹书所说更何如也。

12.8 If one thought of the "dragon and tiger" today and the "water and fire" the next day, and remained in thoughts without actually practising, one would be just a wishful thinker. [42] Previously, I had the chance to receive the oral transmission from Jia De Shen, 贾得升 (more commonly known as the "Fire Dragon Deity"), who also emphasized the importance of practice. Not sure if the text books would emphasize the same.

12.9 一日有一周天，一刻有一周天，坎离交处，便是一周。我之交，即天之回转也，未尝少息。

12.9 There could be one energy cycle in one day. There could be one energy cycle in one moment. At every exchange between the "kan" and "li" trigrams / phenomenons, one energy cycle was completed. Here, in the practitioner's case, the "kan" and "li" exchange might not occur all the time, but the rotating motion of the earth (i.e. energy) continued regardless.

12.10 果能阴阳交泰，人地阳和，我之中宫正位，万物一时畅遂，即丹经沐浴法也。非大周天而何？

---

42   In Taoism, the "dragon and tiger" and the "water and fire" references are all terms for the spirit and essence. The teacher here is trying to bring out the importance of the actual practice rather than mere theoretical understanding.

12.10 Once the "yin" and "yang" energy united harmoniously, and the "zhong gong, 中宫"(i.e. the chest / heart area (middle "dan tian")) was in its rightful position, the entire universe might instantaneously become uninhibitedly forthwith. This was essentially the "mind bath" practice as expounded in the Taoist text. (see Chapter 8) In this regard, wasn't this phenomenon of the "big" energy cycle?[43]

12.11 此中火候，实实有大小不同，究竟无大小可别。

12.11 Here, one might notice different levels of energy cycle (or different degrees of intensity or efficacy). In reality, such distinctions were not necessary.

12.12 到得工夫自然，不知坎离为何物？天地为何等，孰为交，孰为一周两周，何处觅大小之别耶。

12.12 When one gained mastery of the practice, naturally one would no longer know / aware of the "kan" and "li", nor the heaven and earth, whether or not they exchanged and for how long the exchange was. Thus, one need not distinguish between the big or small energy cycle.

12.13 总之一身旋运，虽见得极大亦小，若一回旋，天地万物，悉与之回旋，即在方寸处，亦为极大。

12.13 One point to note for all practitioners. Even if the energy cycle circulated throughout the entire body structure (i.e. the "big" energy cycle), it might still be considered a "small" energy cycle if one did not practice

---

43   Please see the explanation at the beginning of this chapter.

right. On the contrary, even if the energy cycle was circulating in a small part of the body but with the right practice, the universal energy moved in tandem with it, this might indeed be the "big" energy cycle.

12.14 金丹火候，要归自然。不自然，天地自还天地，万物各归万物。欲强之使合，终不能合。

12.14 Therefore, the efficacy of the "golden pill" (see Chapter 1), i.e. levels of attainment by a practitioner, must adhere to the law of nature. Otherwise, the heaven and earth remained the heaven and earth. The universe remained the universe. Both could not be united forcefully.

12.15 即如天时亢旱，阴阳不和。乾坤未尝一日不周，然终见得有多少不自然处。

12.15 For example, during the drought, the "yin" and "yang" energies were out of balance. But the rotation of the earth would continue regardless. It was just somewhat unnatural.

12.16 我能转运阴阳，调适自然，一时云蒸雨降，草木酣适，山河流畅，纵有乖戾，亦觉顿释，此即大周天也。

12.16 In this case, if we "mobilize" the "yin" and "yang" energies and fine-tune them naturally, the sky would start to gather clouds and soon rain would fall to nourish the plants and earth. The rivers would start to flow again. Any state of unnaturalness would soon disappear. This was the actual principle of the "big" energy cycle.

12.17 问活子时甚妙，必认定正子时似着相，不着相不指明正子时。从何识活子时，即识得活子时，确然又有一正子时，是二是一，非正非活，总要人看得真，一真则无不正，无不活矣。

12.17 A question might arise regarding the wonderful experience where the live "yang" energy was activated (see Chapter 8). But, one must establish the right "yang" energy first.[44] Here, one might wonder if the live "yang" energy and the right "yang" energy were essentially the same phenomenon. But, the answer was no. One must establish / identify the right "yang" energy first, so that the phenomenon of live "yang" energy could be perceived / penetrated. In practice, one could witness the activation of the live "yang" energy, but the right "yang" energy would have also manifested alongside. Whether they are the same or different, one should penetrate the truth thoroughly. In the state of ultimate truth, all phenomenons were right and alive.

---

44   For any Taoism or "qi gong" practitioner, the practice is best carried out during the period where the live "yang" energy is activated. This is applicable both in the case of "big" and "small" energy cycles. (In the Chinese term, "huo zi shi, 活子时" literally meant live (huo, 活) midnight (zi shi, 子时). Following the line of thought on the "kan" and "li" trigrams / phenomenon, the midnight reference represented the north pole position, where the real "yang" energy was withdrawn (Chapter 8). Therefore, I have translated "midnight, 子时"as "yang" energy. On the other hand, "zheng si shi, 正子时" (which I translated as right ("zheng, 正")

# Chapter 13: Song of life
# 第十三章：劝世歌[45]

13.1 吕祖曰：

13.1 Lü-zu sang:

13.2 "吾因度世丹中热，不惜婆心并饶舌。

13.2 "For the passion of liberating all sentient beings, I did not hesitate to give discourses repeatedly.

13.3 世尊亦为大因缘，直指生死真可惜。

13.3 Buddha Sakyamuni had pointed out that rolling in the wheel life and death unceasingly due to the karmic cause and effect was regrettably unfortunate for all sentient beings.

13.4 老君也患有吾身，传示谷神人不识。

13.4 The Taoism founding master, Lao Zi also mentioned about bodily afflictions while giving public discourses about the truth and essence of spirit, which the sentient beings failed to grasp.

13.5 吾今略说寻真路

---

[45] For the first half of this chapter, the teacher sang the song of life. Here, my translation was a combination of literal translation as well as the intended meaning behind the lyrics, wherever possible (different from chapter 8, where the poem was first translated literally and explained later).

13.5 Now, let me expound on the path of seeking the ultimate truth:

13.6 黃中通理載大易，正位居体是玄关。

13.6 In I Ching, it was recorded that the heart / mind could access the ultimate truth, provided that it was "rightly located" within the body.[46] Here, apart from the more tangible description, this verse in I Ching also meant having the "right" mind to achieve enlightenment.

13.7 子午中间堪定息，光回祖窍万神安。

13.7 Between midnight and noon, one could meditate to still the breath, light returned to its original abode resulting in peace and calm. If we referred further to the teacher's explanation below, this verse actually described the realization of the exchange between the "kan" and "li" trigrams / phenomenons. In such state, one's breath became still. The essence and spirit would returned to the primordial state. (see Chapter 11)

13.8 药产川原一炁出，透幌变化有金光。

13.8 The medicine (cure) emerged once the energy of life was activated, resulting in the golden light penetrating all veils.

13.9 一轮红日常赫赫，世人错认坎离精。

---

46  The term "huang zhong, 黃中" referred to the heart organ (physical / tangible) and inner virtues (intangible).

13.9 Whenever the bright light was perceived, the humans mistakenly identified such manifestation as the exchange of the "kan" and "li" trigrams / phenomenon.
(See Chapter 10 regarding light with consciousness)

13.10 搬运心肾成间隔，如何人道合天心。

13.10 Moving the attention from the heart at this state, one created an obstacle / barrier to advance further. How to practice in accordance with the universal law of nature?

13.11 天若符兮道自合，放下万缘毫不起。

13.11 One must understand the principle that as and when the universe was aligned, all path to liberation became natural. Here, one must let go of all karmic entanglements and reached the state of non-arising (i.e. no more new creation of karmic entanglements).

13.12 此是先天真无极，太虚穆穆腾朕兆捐。

13.12 This was indeed the primordial state of infinity. One could penetrate such ultimate truth in still meditative state, without any prognostication.

13.13 性命关头忘意识，意识忘后见本真。

13.13 The key to liberation was to forego all thoughts and consciousness (breaking away from all dependencies). The true self emerged once all dependencies were broken.
(See Chapter 10)

13.14 水清珠现玄难测，无始烦障一旦空。玉京降下九龙册，步云汉兮登天关，掌雷霆兮驱霹雳。

13.14 It would be difficult to predict when such state of "clear" mind could be obtained. Once the mind was fully purified, one attained enlightenment. Here, the song further described what would happen at the point of enlightenment. The celestial authority would send the nine dragons, escorting one to rise up to the celestial realm. Having attained enlightenment, one had the ability to manoeuvre the thunderbolt (i.e. gained enormous "power").

13.15 凝神定息是初机，退藏密地为常寂。"

13.15 In conclusion, the energy agglomeration at deep meditative state was the starting point for one to reach the secret abode of all the enlightened ones."

13.16 吾昔度张珍奴二词，皆有大道。

13.16 Previously, when liberating Zhang Zhen Nu (张珍奴), I crafted two verses, which contained the instructions toward enlightenment.[47]

---

47  This is a legendary story between the teacher (Lü-zu, Lü Dong Bin) and Zhang Zhen Nu, a famous prostitute who wanted to leave her trade badly. Lü-zu manifested as a scholar to acquaint himself with her and taught her the path to liberation. The two verses were:
(1) 道无巧妙，与妳方儿一个；子后午前定息坐，夹脊双观昆仑过。这时得气力，思量我。
(2) 坎离震兑分子午，须认取自家宗祖。地雷震动山头雨，带洗濯黄芽出土。捉得金精牢闭固，炼甲庚要生龙虎。待他问汝甚人传？但说道先生姓吕。
The following teaching and detailed explanation quoted on these two verses.

13.17 子后午前非时也，坎离耳。定息者，息息归根，中黄也。坐者，心不动也。夹脊者，非背上轮子，乃直透玉京大路也。双关者，此处有难言者。

13.17 In the first verse, I mentioned about "after midnight, 子后" and "before noon, 午前". Here, I did not mean time but the "kan" and "li" trigrams / phenomenons. For the practitioners, the breath was kept still and rightly fixated at the "huang zhong", i.e. the heart / mind (see above). The heart / mind was also kept still. In the same verse, I referred to the spine of the body, as the metaphor to the path toward the celestial abode of supreme god (i.e. final liberation / enlightenment). The part about "shuang guan, 双关"(literal meaning: double passes) could not be easily explained here.

13.18 地雷震动山头雨者，真气生也。黄芽出土者，药生也。

13.18 In the second verse, the phrase referring to the shattering earth and mountain rain was the metaphor for the emergence / generation of true energy of life (essence). Following that, a sprout grew out from the earth. This was essentially referring to the medicine / cure of life.

13.19 小小二段，已尽修行大路，

13.19 Both these two verses contained the main teaching for the path toward enlightenment.

13.20 明此可不惑人言。

13.20 Understanding them thoroughly, one would not

be easily confused by others.

13.21 昔夫子与颜子登泰山顶，望吴门白马，颜子见为疋练，夫子急掩其目，恐其太用眼力，神光走落，回光可不勉哉！

13.21 Once upon the time, Confucius climbed the Tai Mountain (located in Shandong Province, one of the five great mountains in China) with one of his disciples, Yan Hui. They saw a white horse running across the Wu territory (Wu (229—280), in the Yangtze River Delta, was one of the three major states that competed for supremacy over China in the Three Kingdoms period (220—280)). Yan Hui became very focused on the horse, exclaimed that the trail of the horse was like a piece of white cloth. Confucius quickly covered his eyes so that Yan Hui would not over-exert on his eye function, disallowing the primordial spirit to "flee" away. All light reflex practitioners must take note to avoid such over-exertion.

13.22 回光在纯心行去，只将真息凝照于中宫，久之自然通灵达变也。

13.22 In order to practice the light reflex technique, one should maintain a focused and pure mind in order to agglomerate all essence (breath) in the "zhong gong, 中宫"area, i.e. the chest / heart area (middle "dan tian"). With persistence over time, one would naturally progress to reaching full enlightenment.

13.23 总是心静炁定为基，心忘炁凝为效，炁息心空为丹成，心炁浑一为温养，明心见性为了道。

13.23 In conclusion, one could build the foundation

by having a peaceful mind and a stilled and calm breath. Then, one would progress to witness the benefits of energy agglomeration. Here, the elixir of life could be realized once the breath and mind were united as one. With this, one would be sure on the right path toward enlightenment (see Chapter 4).

13.24 子辈各宜勉力行去，错过光阴可惜也。

13.24 All practitioners should take this practice seriously and persistently. Any waste of time would indeed be regrettable.

13.25 一日不行，一日即鬼也。一息行此，一息真仙也。

13.25 One day without realizing the light reflex, one remained a ghost (Chapter 8). A breath in the state of light reflex, one achieved a moment of true fairy.

13.26 勉之！勉之！"

13.26 May all work hard! May all work diligently.

Printed in Great Britain
by Amazon